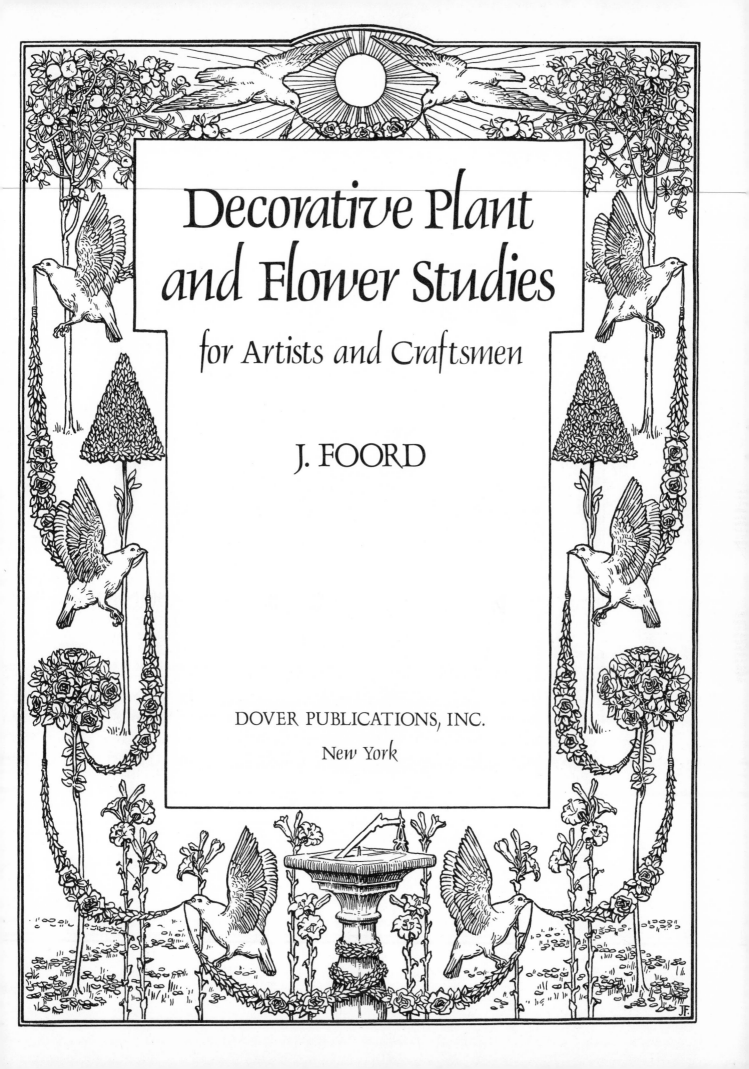

Decorative Plant and Flower Studies

for Artists and Craftsmen

J. FOORD

DOVER PUBLICATIONS, INC.

New York

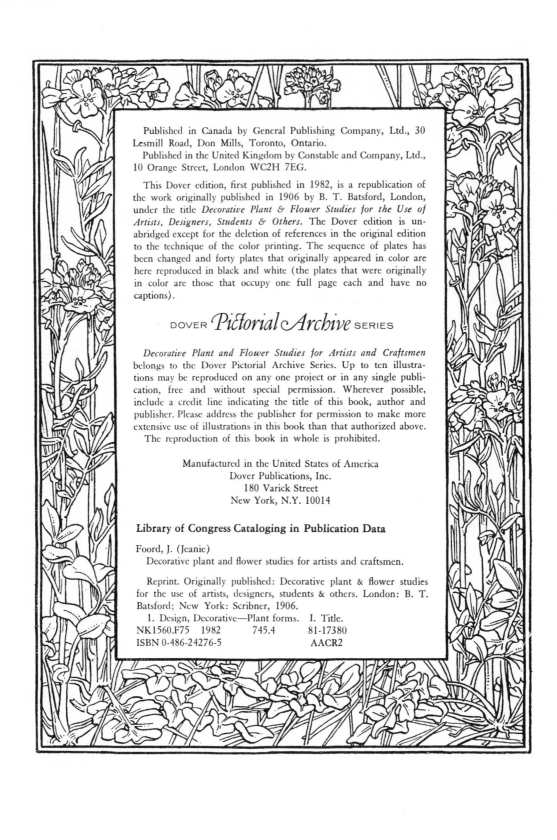

Published in Canada by General Publishing Company, Ltd., 30 Lesmill Road, Don Mills, Toronto, Ontario.

Published in the United Kingdom by Constable and Company, Ltd., 10 Orange Street, London WC2H 7EG.

This Dover edition, first published in 1982, is a republication of the work originally published in 1906 by B. T. Batsford, London, under the title *Decorative Plant & Flower Studies for the Use of Artists, Designers, Students & Others*. The Dover edition is unabridged except for the deletion of references in the original edition to the technique of the color printing. The sequence of plates has been changed and forty plates that originally appeared in color are here reproduced in black and white (the plates that were originally in color are those that occupy one full page each and have no captions).

DOVER *Pictorial Archive* SERIES

Manufactured in the United States of America
Dover Publications, Inc.
180 Varick Street
New York, N.Y. 10014

Library of Congress Cataloging in Publication Data

Foord, J. (Jeanie)
    Decorative plant and flower studies for artists and craftsmen.

    Reprint. Originally published: Decorative plant & flower studies for the use of artists, designers, students & others. London: B. T. Batsford; New York: Scribner, 1906.
    1. Design, Decorative—Plant forms. I. Title.
NK1560.F75   1982   745.4   81-17380
ISBN 0-486-24276-5   AACR2

INTRODUCTORY NOTE
BY MR. LEWIS F. DAY.

BEING, as I believe, partly responsible for Miss Foord undertaking a second series of Plant Studies, I feel called upon to say a word or two by way of introduction to it.

I have had need from time to time of authority for some plant, out of season at the moment, of which I had not made studies, or not studies enough for the purposes of design ; and have been driven—as what designer has not ?—to seek in published illustrations data on which to work. It is not often that I found in prints what I wanted. Drawings which at first sight promised everything proved very often in the end to be of little use. Some were too pictorial in treatment ; some too vague ; they did not as a rule give information enough to go upon, or did not give it definitely. Nothing, of course, will ever take the place of a man's own studies done for his own purpose ; but Miss Foord's drawings came nearer than most to what I wanted ; and it seems only fair to say so, both in her interest and in that of the many to whom such trustworthy studies may be useful.

This new series seems to me an advance upon the first.* I would say that the subjects were better chosen, were it not that I had myself suggested some of them. They cover a wider range—shrubs and trees as well as wild flowers and garden plants—and she has given in every case not only details from which the designer should be able to build up his design, but a suggestive view of the complete plant, showing its growth and general aspect. She has looked at nature with her own eyes, and rendered it faithfully as she saw it ; but it is clear that she has had always in view the wants of students, to whom, according to their proficiency and purpose, they should be equally useful as models of plant form and as materials for design. She has in no case tampered with natural growth or twisted it to her purpose—she has gone no further in decorative treatment than to make careful choice of the most beautiful features of the plant and to render it simply and broadly in outline and flat tints. As documents therefore her studies are to be trusted. They are drawn with care and exactness, and with a firm line there is no mistaking.

In the three years which have passed since the publication of her first series of studies, Miss Foord has improved in draughtsmanship. Her written account of the growth, appearance, and habit of the plants illustrated will help another to make use of them—and if he loves flowers he will find himself reading them again for the pleasure of it, for the way they bring him nearer to nature. As an incentive and inspiration also to those less anxiously in search of new material they may be commended alike to student and amateur.

L. F. D.

*The reference is to an earlier book in the same format, *Decorative Flower Studies,* Batsford, London, 1903.—PUBLISHER, 1982.

AUTHOR'S PREFACE.

IN publishing a second series of Flower Studies, much thought has been given to the selection of subjects, and suggestions have been asked, and most kindly given, from well-known designers, art masters, and others, whose varied knowledge of many branches of crafts-manship should render their opinions of value, not only as to the needs of any one branch of design, but as offering material more or less of use to many.

As far as was possible these suggestions have been carried out, but at the same time I have felt very strongly the difficulty and undesirability of drawing subjects which, while suggesting beauty to some others, have not perhaps appealed in the same way to me, so that through me they carry no message. On the other hand I have included certain flowers which may have been deemed unimportant, but whose decorative value has impressed me in the fields and hedges and in humble kitchen gardens, such for instance as the " Salsify." But it must not be thought that in putting these studies forward I have the smallest intention of offering them as a substitute to any one for drawing directly from nature, but rather as a means of reference and additional help when that is difficult or impossible ; and, to such students as have not already done so, rather as an incentive to them to seek nature for themselves.

It is not the aim of these drawings to give a naturalistic pictorial view of the plant, but rather that by simple and severe treatment of line the whole strength, delicacy, and character of the form should be expressed, as is most necessary for all practical purposes, retaining as much as is possible of the grace and charm of the flower ; the colour being merely implied or suggested by flat washes which should give an impression of the subject as seen in light and air, and not merely a map of the local colour.* Care has been taken to make the sketches of detail as full and complete as possible, and in giving a small drawing of the whole plant, to find a typical example ; this, however, was not always easy to determine, plants of the same species varying so much in character and growth under different conditions.

In all cases the subjects are drawn as they grow, the line being absolutely as in nature, such decorative effect as they may have being due to careful selection and placing on the page, and not to any sacrifice of the form ; and where any adjunct is given, as in the case of the stems of grass in the drawing of Rest Harrow, it is given not merely to form a pleasing page, but to show further the habits and scale of the plant in its almost invariable environment.

I would express grateful thanks to many who have given me very kind help, and to acknowledge especially how much I owe to the reliable judgment and most valuable advice of the late Mr. Bradley Batsford, always most kindly and freely given.

Lastly, I must express my indebtedness to the simply expressed personal knowledge and quaint beliefs of the early English herbalists, who wrote with such an intimate touch and real love of their subjects. As for example, William Cole, in his preface to "Adam in Eden," published in 1657, says, "When God Almighty would have Adam to partake of a perfection of happinesse, even then when he stood innocent, he could find none greater under the sun than to place him in a Garden."

J. FOORD.

LONDON, *October,* 1906.

*This pale and nonnaturalistic color is omitted in the present edition.—PUBLISHER, 1982.

CONTENTS

APPLE BLOSSOM.

Nat. Ord. *Rosaceæ*

FEW of our English flowers are richer in decorative qualities than the various fruit blossoms : the apple, the cherry, the pear, and the plum all being so full of delicate beauty, both of form and colour, that it is difficult to give preference to either ; while some of the many varieties of the black thorn in our hedges are quite equal to the cultivated trees in the material they offer to the designer. Among these the apple has perhaps an advantage in coming rather later than the others, when the young foliage has already made considerable growth, so that its flowers are set among the fresh soft green

of the young leaves instead of on bare stems, and also that it has a more clustered arrangement than the plum or the black-thorn, the flowers springing from the branch in well grouped masses surrounded by the radiating foliage, instead of in their more scattered growth.

The apple does not often grow to a great height, but old trees sometimes reach thirty or thirty-five feet ; occasionally even more. The growth is full of character, the gnarled grey stems dividing into twisted knotted branches, which spread in a more or less horizontal direction, often with a pendulous droop in the smaller boughs at the extremities. The young trees are generally more erect, but the growth differs slightly in different varieties, though all retain the same general characteristics. The drawing of the stems is full of interest and delicate form, with sudden turns and sharp angles, and with the thickened ringed bark at the joints. The leaves are ovate, tapering to a point, with flexible stems which give a valuable effect of looseness in the clustered grouping ; the edges are irregularly serrated, the netted veining strong and clear, and the lower sides of the leaves are soft and woolly, and of a pale grey, contrasting with the stronger colour of the upper surface. In the young leaves, as seen at the time of the blossom, this is of a bright fresh green, but later they grow much darker, and greyer and more reserved in colour. On the young shoots their order is generally alternate, but in the older growth it is irregular, forming clusters of radiating leaves surrounding the flowers, or leafy terminals in which the beautiful folding of the opening leaves should be noticed, and the long pointed bracts at the base of the stalk.

The flowers grow in well-massed umbels, those in the centre being the first to open, surrounded by later buds. Each blossom has five long pointed sepals which are folded over the bud, then, opening with the flower, gradually become reflexed, lying back against the stem ; five concave petals, opening out to a broad cup-shaped corolla, in the centre of which is the soft loose fringe of stamens and anthers. The petals are of a silky semi-transparent texture, and the whole flower is beautifully delicate in colour, the corolla of a faint shell-like pink, splashed at the edges, on the outer side only, with a deeper rose, the buds being often entirely flushed with the darker tone ; while the calyx, with the stems or pedicels, is of a pale green softened with a covering of velvety down ; in the centre of the flower the loose fringed anthers give a suggestion of palest yellow, deepening as it fades, and the whole dainty mass of the umbel of blossom is set in the soft fresh green of the surrounding leaves.

The apple is the most typically English of all our fruits, and flourishes and comes to its greatest perfection in all parts of the British Isles. Hereford, Worcester, and to a less extent Devonshire are the principal apple producing counties of the present day, but Gerard, in 1509, states that they were especially plentiful in Kent, and both he and Parkinson write of an "infinite number of varieties, and of many medicinal virtues and quaint uses." The crab and several other wild apples are indigenous, and not uncommon in our hedges, in fact the apple grows more or less freely in all parts of Europe, excepting in extremes of heat and cold, as well as in parts of North America, Western Asia, and in China and Japan. It is known to have been largely cultivated in the neighbourhood of Rome, and is supposed to have been introduced into England by the Romans ; it is mentioned frequently in their writings, as well as in those of the Greeks. It was offered on the altars of Hercules ; later it was worshipped by the Druids with the oak, in connection with the sacred mistletoe ; and we read of it in many old legends, in the well-known mythological tales of the golden apples,—or oranges,—of the Garden of the Hesperides, the Judgment of Paris, etc. ; in old Norse and Scandinavian folklore, and in many quaint stories and superstitions of later mediæval times.

Both the flowers and fruit have been largely used in decorative art ; the former, with all the fruit blossoms, especially and most worthily, by the Japanese ; in our modern western design it has suffered greatly from hackneyed and unstudied mediocre renderings, but it still offers endless opportunities in the hands of conscientious workers, who realize its greater dignity and charm in a more severe and truthful rendering.

APPLE BLOSSOM.

1, 2, 3, 4, 5, 6. Stages of the opening buds.　7. Flower.　8. Growth of flowers and buds.
9. Calyx, with stamens and pistil after the fall of the petals.　10. Lateral leaf growth.　11. Jointed
branch.　12. Back view of the flower.　13. Petals.

Sketch of Fruit.

THE EVENING PRIMROSE.

Nat. Ord. *Onagraceæ.*

THE Evening Primrose is one of the commonest of our garden flowers, and one that in broad day-light attracts but little notice, with its tall spikes of closed or fading blossoms. But in the evening, when many other flowers are closing, if we stand and watch it for a little time we see first one and then another of the closed buds suddenly unseal the enclosing sepals and fold them back, and quite visibly and quickly, while we watch, the bud expands, the folded petals gradually loosen, and in a few minutes the big cup-like blossom appears fully opened and in all the beauty of its most delicate colour, the pure light gold of the flowers gleaming pale in the soft grey of the dusk, and shedding a faint subtle scent on the still dew-laden air.

But apart from its charm of pure delicate colour, and the illusive beauty of the twilight effect, the Evening Primrose has also much of the real decorative quality of beauty of form. The large well opened blossom, with the long sepals turned back with quaint effect, the tall spikes of buds and flowers, and the simple undulating leaves are rich in suggestion.

The herbaceous plant rises from a cluster of radical leaves with a tall straight stem, generally erect, but not rigidly ver-tical, sending out lateral branches, each also terminated with spikes of blossom. These give a certain bushy effect, but the central spike always rises above them forming a dis-tinct head. The leaves are lanceolate-elliptical, with strong clearly marked midrib, the edges simple, but the surface more or less undulating ; from the axils of the leaves the lateral branches and the blossoms of the flower-spikes spring. The tapering bud is enclosed in the long segments of the calyx, which form a valuable decorative feature of the open flower ; the corolla consists of four large petals, inversely deltoid ; these enclose eight anthers on long slender stamens, and a projecting cruciform stigma on a long style. The flower is sessile, having no stem, though at first sight this is not very evident, owing to the stem-like effect of the long tube of the calyx running down to the ovary or seed-vessel, which is closely set in the axil of the leaf. A section of this calyx-tube is shown in the page of detail drawings. The seed-vessel remains long after the flower has fallen, and grows to about one-and-a-half inches in length. As the lower blossoms fall, fresh buds develope and open above, forming a continu-ally growing spike, and giving a long succession of blossom, although the life of each individual flower lasts only a few hours. The plant grows to a height of from four to six feet, and the radical leaves are from six to twelve inches in length, while those of the stem are from three to six inches long.

The evening primrose is a native of North America, but it is now very common in English gardens, where it quickly spreads ; and in some few places, especially on the Lancashire coast, it has established itself as a wild flower, growing in great patches on bits of waste land and common, and forming, even in broad daylight, when comparatively few of the flowers remain open, a beautiful harmony of pale gold set in the deep dull green of the foliage, relieved by the lighter tracery of the stems and the valuable note of deep soft orange in the fading blossoms.

1, 2, 3. Buds.   4. Opening flower.   5. Showing growth of the flowers.   6. Flower with petals removed showing growth of stamens and pistil.   7. Section of the calyx tube.   8. Seed vessel.   9. Section of seed vessel.   10. Part of main stem showing growth of flowering branches.

PYRUS SPECTABILIS.

Nat. Ord., *Rosaceæ*.

PART of the large order of the Rosaceæ, the genus Pyrus, the old Latin name for the Pear Tree, now embraces not only the very decorative and useful pear and apple, but also a large number of beautiful hybrid flowering trees and shrubs, of which Pyrus Spectabilis may be taken as one of the finest and most representative. It has all the airy lightness of growth of the pear or cherry blossom, throwing out spreading umbels of dainty long-stemmed flowers, more or less drooping, among the fresh vivid green of the young leaves ; and at the same time the delicate colouring of the apple, a pale shell-like pink, splashed on the outer side of the thin semi-transparent petals with a slightly deeper tone, while the light fringe of long-stamened anthers give a faint suggestion of soft yellow in the centre of the flower. With the delicate petals, however, the resemblance ceases, the calyx and stems taking a deep bronze where the rose mingles with the green, forming a telling contrast to the paler tones, while the leaves are of a strong warm yellowish green, fresh and brilliant, and of a pale glaucous colour on the lower surface, the stems of the older wood being of a light ashen grey.

Like so many of the most beautiful of our flowering shrubs, it is of Eastern origin, growing in China and Japan, and was brought to us from the former country in 1780. It grows freely in England, sometimes in sheltered positions, attaining a height of from twenty to thirty feet, sometimes under less favourable conditions, taking a lower and more branching growth, and remaining merely a bushy shrub. As a standard tree it rises with straight strong trunk, and, at from three to five feet from the ground, divides into spreading branches, which again send out numerous long flexible lateral shoots, each thickly set in early spring with the clustering pendulous masses of mingled flowers and leaves.

The umbels of blossom grow from short spurs set at close intervals on the branches, forming long swaying wreaths of flowers and foliage, each blossom on its long flexible stalk supported by a blunt five-toothed calyx. It is semi-double, and the numerous ovate incurved petals taper to a slender pointed inguis, or hooked terminal, at their base, this thread-like tapering attachment giving the great effect of looseness and buoyancy, which is such a strong characteristic of the flower, and such a valuable quality from a decorative point of view. The buds are of the typical rosaceæ form ; the incurved petals folded over each other taking a close globular shape supported and held together by the enclosing segments of the toothed calyx which rise from the ovary. The buds are generally erect, but sway and droop as the petals unfold and the flowers gain weight, keeping as they open rather the spherical form of the pear blossom than that of the wider, flatter flower of the apple. The lanceolate leaves, also with long lissom stems, are of decided ovate shape, more or less blunt and square at the apex, with curling incurved edges irregularly serrated, and billowy undulating surface ; the veining being clearly marked, and forming thick raised cords on the lower

surface. The colour is a strong, warm, yellowish green, much paler and greyer on the reverse of the leaf. The shrub blooms very freely, producing a profusion of delicate pink and white blossoms in April or May ; these, however, quickly fall, the light petals being scattered by the wind, and in common with other semi-double hybrids, it does not produce fruit.

With its clustering well-massed growth of flowers and leaves, its radiating flexible stems, and the interest and charm of the well-opened blossoms, Pyrus Spectabilis seems peculiarly rich in the decorative qualities which are of value to the designer.

PYRUS SPECTABILIS.

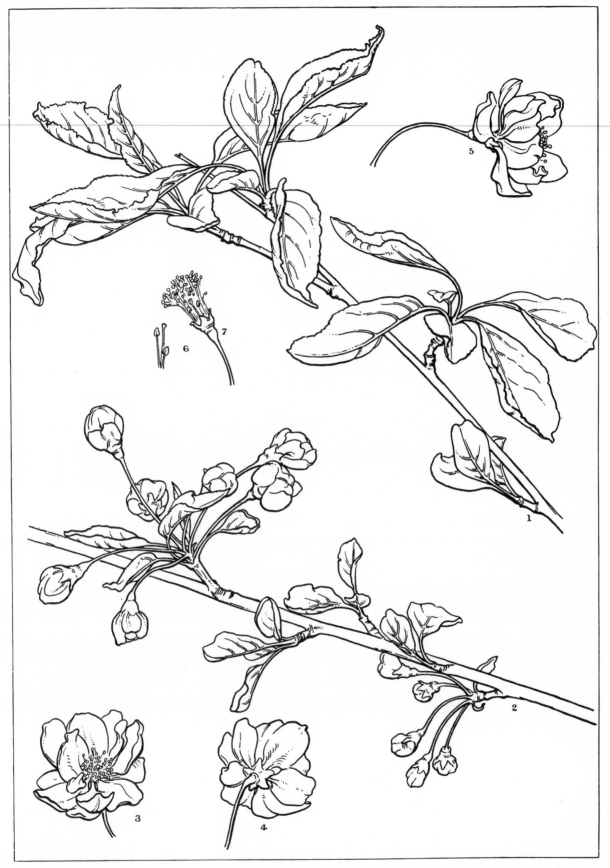

1. General growth of the leaves.   2. Buds in different stages, showing their growth.   3. Front view of the flower.   4. Back view of the flower.   5. Flower in profile.   6. Stamens.   7. Calyx, showing growth of the stamens.

THE DAFFODIL.

Nat. Ord., *Amaryllidaceæ.*

THE name Daffodil is simply a corruption of the old English "affo dyle," meaning "that which cometh early"; and it is very early in the spring, or rather almost in the late winter, that the first of its pale green spikes may be seen pushing up through the moist brown earth in our gardens, and in many parts of England in our woods and meadows. The root is a bulb, with smooth pale brown outer covering which is carried up forming a dry scarious sheath protecting the young leaves. From each sheath, of which there may be two or more to a bulb, spring two or three flat green leaves, closely packed together, and rising in a strictly vertical direction until they have attained about two-thirds of their height. Then they take freer, more swaying lines, and from between them the tall straight scape or flower stem appears, with its terminal bud. The leaves are straight-veined, linear or strap-shaped, tapering towards the rounded point, and from twelve to eighteen inches high. The flower stem, which rises a little above the leaves, is strong and thick, the upper part flattened with two well-marked angles running down its length. The bud is enclosed in a protecting green spathe, but as the flower unfolds, this becomes dry and scarious, and takes a thin transparent texture. At first it is erect, but, as it opens it becomes depressed, till in the flower the axis is more or less horizontal or drooping. The blossom consists of a perianth tube rising from the ovary, with six spreading perianth segments; within which the crown, which in the Narcissus is flat and cup-shaped, is in the Daffodil lengthened to a long trumpet-shaped funnel, which at the apex expands with a graceful spreading curve, the edge being curled and crenulated, and rather reflexed. Within the funnel and attached to its sides at the base, are six long stamens with large anthers, and a long style with three-partite stigma.

The Daffodil is one of the most popular of our spring flowers, and in every garden, in March, "the roaring month of daffodils," the tremulous yellow blossoms, so delicate and fragile, will be seen swaying and tossing above the long straight wind-swept leaves; while more especially in the south-western counties, where it is found in rich profusion as a wild flower,—growing in woods and sheltered copses, on the river banks, and in the open fields,—it spreads in great flowery stretches, shining brilliant in the sunlight, and forming innumerable star-like dots of pale colour in the shadows. The leaves are of a beautiful subtle grey-green, while the outer segments of the flower are of the palest yellow, and the long inner tube is of a deep rich gold. The general effect is of a scheme of upright growth, yet with strong sweeping graceful lines that prevent any severe effect, and the whole plant is beautifully balanced, and full of decorative feeling.

Only the short-crowned yellow variety and the pheasant's eye seem to have been known to the Greeks and Romans, but in the sixteenth and early seventeenth centuries there were many varieties; and Gerard, Parkinson, and Tradescant, that earnest trio of lovers of nature, all cultivated them enthusiastically in their gardens in Holborn and Chelsea, producing many new varieties. We read that we are indebted to Tradescant for the large double daffodil, or "Lent Lily," which was known as " John Tradescant, his great rose daffodil." Another was " Gerard's double daffodil " ; and of his own Parkinson writes lovingly : " I think none ever had this kinde before myself, nor did I myself ever see it before the year 1618, for it is of mine own raising and flowring in my garden." But it is evident that this noted trio of herbalists, generally unanimous, had differences of opinion about the daffodil, Gerard vouching for its medicinal virtues, " as hath been prooued by an especial and trusted friend of mine, a man learned, and a diligent searcher of nature, Master Nicholas Belson, sometimes of King's Colledge, in Cambridge " ; while Parkinson writing later, says of the species : " Howsoever Dioscorides and others doe give vnto some of them special properties both for inward and outward diseases, yet know I not any in these days with vs, that apply any of them as a remedy for any griefe, whatsoever Gerrard or others have written."

There are now innumerable varieties of the Daffodil, many imported from Southern Europe and especially from Spain, others the result of modern cultivation. They vary greatly in depth and strength of colour, and especially in size, but the well-known garden single Daffodil, and the wild variety, smaller, lighter, and more delicate in structure than the heavier and more massive blossoms of many of the most choice cultivated flowers, remain to the artist among the most desirable.

1, 2, 3, 4. Stages of opening buds.   5, 6. Leaf and flower, showing relative height.   7. Front view of flower.   8. Section showing structure.   9, 10. Leaf terminations.   11. Sheath.   12. Bulb and roots.
13. Section of flower scape or stem.

BROOM.

Nat. Ord., *Leguminaceæ*.

"Along the copses runs in veins of gold."

THE Broom, plante-de-genista, is found over the greater part of Western and Southern Europe, and is one of our native English shrubs, growing freely on many of our commons and pieces of waste land, and on any sunny sandy banks where it may flourish undisturbed. Sometimes in low, almost prostrate, bushes; sometimes rising in thick masses to a height of from six to about ten feet, it gives, in May and June, such a profusion of flowers that the whole of the great stretches of bushy growth are a blaze of pendant golden blossom. Following the fallen fruit blossoms, it is a favourite honey flower for the bees, and their droning musical hum may be heard all day in the green depths of the thick flower-strewn bushes.

Sometimes upright, sometimes with a swinging lateral direction, the plant is built up of numerous straight slender branches, arranged in many swaying parallel lines. The tough fibrous stems are square with sharp angles; throwing out small ovate leaves, some solitary, some tri-foliate, with simple non-serrated edges. In their axils, at the extremities of the branches, the large loose flowers are thickly set, forming long panicles of blossom, their short stems, or pedicels, being so slender and flexible as to give a more or less drooping loose effect. They have the usual structure of all the papillionaceous flowers, the standard, large and rather incurved, two loose wings with their curious hooked attachment, and a curved heel, from which the long stamens project in long upward lines, supporting the anthers. After the flower has fallen the persistent calyx remains with these stamens enclosed in a delicate membranous sheath, from which the small green pod, or seed-vessel, presently emerges. This is covered and fringed at the edges with a delicate ciliation of downy hairs, growing loosely, softening the outlines and shedding a cool grey tone over the pale fresh green. These pods grow to a length of from two to two-and-a-half inches, taking a decided curve in direction which is continued in the long style remaining at their apex; while the scarious membranous sheath in which the stamens were enclosed, still protects the base, attached to the calyx. As the pods ripen they also become scarious, and change colour to a deep bluish-purple; and as they are usually very numerous, the plant in this stage, although with quite a different and less brilliant effect of subtle colour, is almost as beautiful as in the flowering season, shining in metallic greys and blues as they catch the light. Finally the pod opens, scattering the seeds, and the two split segments take sharp spiral curves. The seeds are usually ripened in August, and the flowers and purple pods are not seen in conjunction.

The general colour of the flower is a pure golden yellow, very vivid and brilliant, contrasting with the deep sombre green of the leaves and stems, relieved only in early summer with the lighter tone of the young foliage and growing pods. In some varieties the yellow is paler, and in some of the cultivated plants the blossom is in light creamy tones and pure white, but in these it is small and comparatively insignificant without the strong form of the wild flower.

The bushy parallel branches were formerly much used in making brooms, which, previously known as besoms, took their present name from this shrub. In spite of this frequent use of the plant, the yellow flowers were considered of ill omen, and we are told that it was unlucky, and a sign of death, to carry them into a house, a superstition it shared with the hawthorn. An old saying, quoted by Thistleton Dwyer in the "Folklore of Plants," runs—

"If you sweep the house with blossomed broom in May
You are sure to sweep the head of the house away."

At the same time a plentiful flowering of the broom was welcomed as predicting a good harvest.

The Broom is found in mediæval decorative art, and has been largely used in heraldry. Its well-known use as the badge of the Plantagenets need hardly be mentioned. It had long been a favourite emblem in France, and was borne as a symbol of humility by the pilgrims, notably by Fulke, Earl of Anjou, when on a journey to the Holy Land. It was the badge of Bretagne, and on that account was assumed by Henry when laying claim to that province. And in English ornament, we find it valued not for the flower alone, a broom plant with empty pods being seen on the tomb of Richard II in Westminster Abbey.

The name Broom is derived from the old English "brame;" also the origin of the word "bramble."

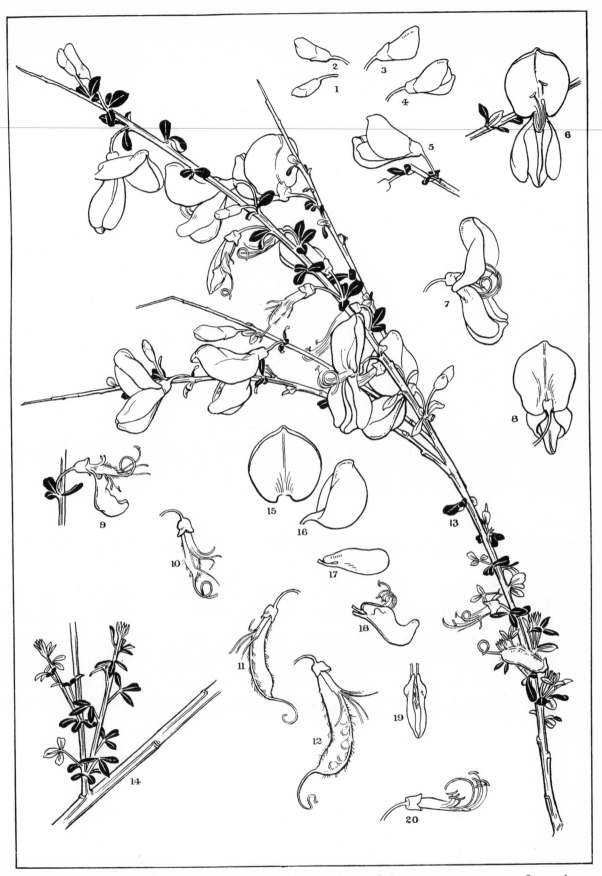

1, 2, 3, 4, 5. Buds.   6, 7, 8. Front view, side, and back of flower.   9, 10, 11, 12. Successive stages of the seed pod.   13. Spray showing general growth of flowers and leaves.   14. Main stem with young lateral shoots.   15, 16. Front and side views of standard.   17. Wing. 18, 19. Side and front view of keel.   20. Calyx, with sheathed stamens and style.

THE FLOWERING RUSH.

Nat. Ord., *Alismaceæ*.

THE Flowering Rush, *Butomus umbellatus*, found only too rarely in England, is one of the most delicately beautiful of our water plants. One feels at once a certain resemblance to the arrowhead, which is of the same order. Although not structurally alike, there is the same effect of dainty pale blossoms on long upright stems, rising from the dusky depths of deep still water, and overhanging its reflecting surface. The same effect of length of line, even longer and more strong and sweeping in the flowering rush than in the arrowhead, and also a certain similarity of colour. And, like the

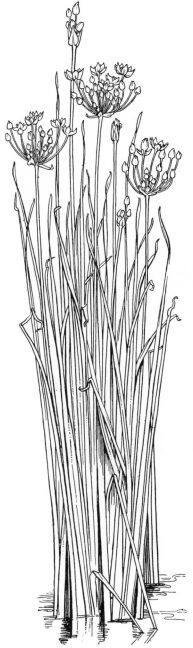

arrowhead, it is very seldom found ; only in the most secluded parts of our English rivers, and in isolated marshes, ponds and ditches its delicate blossoms may be seen, generally well out of reach from the bank.

From the root, which is a thick fleshy creeping rhizome, the long linear leaves rise vertically, forming a dense mass of grassy foliage. Here and there one taller than the rest shoots up side by side with the flowers, but the general mass is some inches below them, and the sheathed buds are seen gradually pushing up from its sheltering cover. The first effect of this mass of green is of a vigorous upright growth ; but looking at each separate leaf it will be seen to turn on its axis in a spiral curve, so that its direction is never severely straight, but in long swaying interlacing lines. It is of sharply marked triangular shape, and though at the base it broadens out into a sheathing surface enveloping the scape and inner leaves, and at the apex it is again slightly flattened, the triangular form is still very apparent throughout. The three sections of the leaf, nos. 9, 10, 11, on the page of drawings of detail will explain this difference of form at the various elevations.

The blossom is an umbel, a spreading head of buds and flowers at the top of a tall round stem usually of absolutely perpendicular growth. In bud it is enclosed in a sheathing involucre of three scarious leaves of a warm brown, tinged more or less with purple. From this the flowers gradually emerge, on separate flower stalks or pedicels, from two to four inches long. The flowers are from threequarters to an inch across, and consist of six very concave perianth segments, the inner three much smaller than the three outer ; white tinged with rose, with markings of a deep soft rose colour on the outer side ; the anthers and ovary being of the same soft dull red. After the flower has withered, the shrivelled perianth remains surrounding the ovary, which consists of six follicles, now much enlarged, with long beaks formed by the persistent style. Each follicle is filled with numerous seeds. The plant grows to a height of from two to four feet, and is in flower through June and July.

Butomus umbellatus is not correctly a rush, but is said to have received its name from the resemblance of its long straight stem to that of the bulrush. The name *Butomus* is derived from *bous* = an ox, and *temno* = to cut, in reference to the sharp leaves which hurt the mouths of cattle. Gerard suggests the name " Lillie Grasse," calling it also " Water Gladiole, or Grassie Rush," and says that " of all others it is the fairest and most pleasant to behold, and serveth very well for the decking and trimming up of houses, because of the beauty and bravery thereof, etc."

1. Buds.   2. General growth of the bud.   3. General growth of the flower.   4. Plan of the flower.
5. Reverse of the flower.   6. Stamens and capsules.   7. Successive stages of the stamens.   8. Leaf.
9, 10, 11. Sections of the leaf at the apex, centre and base.   12. Showing growth of the leaves and
creeping root.

THE TULIP TREE.

Liriodendron. Nat. Ord., *Magnoliaceæ.*

THE Tulip Tree is unfortunately comparatively rare in England, although it grows freely in any slightly sheltered position, equalling our large forest trees in height and in the luxuriant growth of its handsome foliage; while in June and July nearly every branch and spray is set with the beautiful big cup-like flowers, shedding a faint subtle scent.

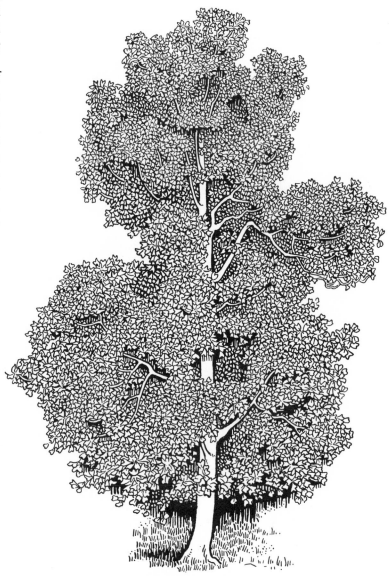

It is found in many parts of central and southern Europe, and in England and Ireland, growing from seventy-five to one hundred feet high; while in its native America, in the western states where it especially flourishes and is very plentiful, it often rises to a hundred-and-forty feet. There it is valued not only for its beauty, since the timber, known as "white wood" from its colour, is very largely used for building and many other practical purposes. The Indians made canoes from it, naming it "canoe wood"; it is also known as the "saddle tree," from the curious shape of the leaf, and "tulip tree," from the lily-like structure of the six-petalled flower. Liriodendron is from leirion = a lily, and dendron = a tree. It is also sometimes spoken of as a poplar, its manner of growth, tall and erect, being very like that tree, and also the plane. The exact date of its introduction into England is not certain, though most authorities give it as 1688, since it was known to have been growing at Fulham at that time. Evelyn suggests that we owe it to John Tradescant, who imported several of our favourite garden flowers from America, but no mention is made of it in the herbals of his contemporaries and friends; the last of these, however, was published nine years before the date of his death, so that this remains a very probable theory.

No plant is more characteristic than the tulip tree, it is one of a mono-typic genus, the only representative of its species, and its individualities are strongly marked. The curious shape of the leaves is peculiarly its own. They are three-lobed, the two lateral being rounded to a point, while the terminal is truncated, sharply cut across, forming a blunt square apex, unlike any other leaf form. They have long slender stems much enlarged at the base, simple uncut edges, the surface flat and smooth, showing clearly the well-marked veining. And not only in form, but in their development, they differ from all others. The flat oval leaf-bud is enclosed in two bract-like scales pressed closely together, between which the young leaf lies folded lengthwise, the long stem and mid-rib bent in a circular curve back to the base. Not until it is well developed do the enclosing scales open, when the long stem, quickly straightening, thrusts out the unfolding leaf, now of considerable size. The bracts remain for a short time as stipules at the base of the stem, where another bud on a short supporting spur is already formed, going quickly through the same process, and producing still another as the second leaf emerges, and yet others following. This curious system of leaf development is shown in the drawings of detail.

The flowers are large and, in the older trees, very numerous; the younger do not blossom freely. At first sight the resemblance to the tulip is more in the shape of the bud than in the flower, although the arrangement of the six petals gives that similarity of structure to all the Liliaceæ from which the tree is named. As the bud opens the three long linear sepals fold back with quaint effect over the stem, on which, just below the blossom, are two small leaf-like bracts. The six petals, three outer and three inner, form a large gradually spreading cup, within which the long erect stamens supporting the large anthers surround the central fruit spike. This is formed of an upright column, to which are attached many overlapping scales, within which are the carpels, each containing two winged seeds.

And not only in its form, growth, and development, but in colour, also, the flower is strange and unusual; the petals are of a pale warm yellow, or maize-colour, with markings at the base of deeper orange, of a beautiful soft quality rather than brilliant; the anthers are of the same rich quiet tone, while the central spike and drooping sepals are of a delicate green. With the strong warm green of the leaves, and the glaucous bluish-grey of their lower surface, it forms a very beautiful colour harmony, rich and reserved; while its varied form, so strong and unusual, offers many opportunities, and, to a certain extent, fresh material to the student. Possibly to some extent its unfamiliarity is a drawback, but its real decorative qualities do not seem to have been fully recognized in applied art, although Mr. Lewis Day has used its broad flat masses most happily in a very strong and beautiful design for a tile.

1, 2, 3. Successive stages of the buds. 4. Opening bud. 5. Flower in early stage. 6. Growth of stamens and stigma in the centre of the flower. 7. Stamen. 8. Stigma. 9. Terminal leaf bud. 9a. Section of bud, showing the growth of the young leaf and bud within. 10, 11. Later stages of the leaf bud. 12, 13. Leaves.

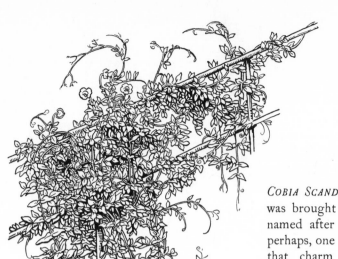

COBIA SCANDENS.

Nat. Ord., *Polemoniaceæ*.

COBIA SCANDENS is a native of Central America, and was brought to us from Mexico in 1792. It was named after the Spanish botanist Cobo. It is not, perhaps, one of those plants which appeal to us from that charm of familiarity and sentiment which attaches to so many of our well known flowers ; a sentiment which often has a distinct commercial value to a designer, quite apart from any quality of beauty either of form or colour ; but simply on the merits of its real decorative qualities that it may be included in any series of studies of plant-form. With a certain quaintness, and with something, perhaps, bordering on the gro-tesque, it seems reminiscent of some old chintz patterns with their flamboyant peonies and tulips. So full of decorative arrangement is it, that the very way it grows, in long loose hanging branches, flowering alternately on each side of the slender swaying stem, each blossom supported by its clustering leaf growth, seems to suggest pattern almost ready made ; and although the long slender branches are often falling, the bearing of each blossom is erect, and the general effect is rather of an upward growth, full of spring and elasticity.

In every stage, from the bud to the last stage of the persistent calyx, the flower seems rich in decorative qualities. Notice the beautiful folding of the bud, with the radiating curves of the large sepals ; then as they open, the large tubular corolla emerges, set in the centre of the wide spreading calyx, and, gradually expanding, reveals the heavy projecting anthers on their long thick stamens, and the still more prominent style. Its broad open tube is divided at the edges into five blunt rounded lobes. As the flower fades, this tubular corolla falls, but the large persistent calyx remains, looking almost like a second form of blossom, with its spreading triply-keeled sepals, undulated at the edges. The colour of the corolla is a deep rich purple, fading into a pale green at the base, while the anthers are of a soft golden yellow ; the calyx repeating the delicate green of the corolla, flushed with a faint suggestion of the deeper purple. The curious thick stalk supporting the flower is noticeable, springing as it does from the slender wiry stem of the branch, which is much thinner and very flexible, though slightly enlarged and square at the joints, where it takes sharp alternating changes of direction.

No less than the flower, the compound leaves also are characteristic and unusual in their growth. Each consists of two or three pairs of leaflets, with a long triply-branched terminal tendril, generally closely curled in tight spiral curves. These pairs of leaflets are not opposite, but spring both from the same side of the stem, twisting over each other, and forming a curious knotted joint. They are of simple elliptical form, with edges entire, and veining strongly and clearly marked. The leaves and flowers are placed alternately on the main stem, the order being strictly kept. The growth of small foliage near the base of the petiole or flower stalk should be noticed, each leaf terminated with a delicate tendril.

The plant is semi-hardy, and grows luxuriantly and very rapidly in any sheltered corners of our gardens, covering old walls or rockwork, or climbing over trellis or the branching stumps of trees. It flowers freely, producing a profusion of blossom through the summer and early autumn, but cannot stand against an English winter, and dies at the first severe frost. In the shelter of a cool house it will live for a long time. Its growth is like that of the passion flower or clematis, climbing with long twisted stems, rising sometimes to a height of thirty or forty feet, and hanging in heavy tangled masses. This climbing swinging pendant growth, in conjunction with the erect bearing of the flowers and the great variety of their form, with the clustering masses of leaves and tendrils, makes it exceedingly adaptable, and full of interest and practical value to designers and students of plant-form.

COBIA SCANDENS.

1, 2, 3. Buds.   4. Back view of the flower.   5. Calyx after fall of the tubular corolla.   6. Showing growth of leaf and thickened flower stalk from slender main stem.   7. Showing leaf growth on the flower stem.   8. Showing growth of pistil, stamens, and anthers.   9. Plan of flower centre.   10. Part of petiole or leaf stalk, showing the growth of the leaves from one side of the stalk.

THE HOLLYHOCK.

Althea rosea.   Nat. Ord., *Malvaceæ.*

To all students of plant-form the close relationship of the Hollyhock with the wild mallows of our fields and hedges is at once apparent, and in their general form and structure they are very similar, while even the great charm of colour of the cultivated plant is shared by some of the wild varieties, notably by the delicate pink and white "marsh mallow." In many beautiful old-fashioned gardens the Hollyhock has long been one of the most striking features, and there is something stately and almost regal in its tall upright spikes of blossom and the vigorous growth of its thick straight stems and large spreading leaves. It has that quality of strength and breadth, of "bigness" in the firm lines of its somewhat massive form which is almost statuesque, and which is so valuable from a decorative point of view; and at the same time an infinite variety of delicate detail with a constant change of plane and subtle differences of texture. And in colour also it has a wide range, from pure white, sometimes blended with faint mauve or lilac shades, soft sulphur yellows, pale pink and deeper rose, to rich wine colour and the darkest crimson and purple; and all these seen in conjunction with the light green stems and the darker neutral colour of the leaves, softened by the thick short down which, excepting the flowers, covers the whole surface of the plant, giving a subtle grey tone and thick woolly texture.

It is a perennial herb, growing from six to ten feet high, while from about three feet above the ground it gives a long succession of flowers, which, though short-lived, are continually replaced by fresh opening buds tending gradually upwards on the long tapering stem. This main stem, thick, strong and erect, is sometimes simple, but often throws out short lateral branches which each produce terminal flower heads, forming a more or less spreading bushy growth, but never rising to the height of the central stem, which remains always the distinct head. The lower leaves are large and round, slightly lobed, with long straight stalks or petioles, their surface billowy and undulating between the strongly-marked palmate and netted veining, the edges irregularly serrated. On the upper stem the leaf-stalks gradually shorten, the leaves taking a longer and more angular form, with three or five short lobes. The flowers grow on short thick stems from the axil of each leaf, either solitary or in groups of two or three. The buds are enclosed in an epicalyx of short pointed linear leaves, folding over the longer inner sepals of the calyx, which are also linear and sharply pointed. The corolla consists of five large wedge-shaped petals, with inturned undulating edges, surrounding the close columnar mass of short stamens and style of about equal length. In the single variety the flower forms a broad spreading cup, in the double the corolla encloses a soft mass of smaller petals, closely packed and crushed together with a rose-like effect. The blossom is followed by the broad flat carpels or seed vessels, enclosed in the persistent calyx, which, as the flowers fall, are left in a long succession on the lengthening flower spike. After the seed is ripened, the stem dies, but the root survives, and sends up fresh flowering shoots in the following spring.

SEED VESSELS.

The Hollyhock blooms from midsummer till late autumn, in sheltered positions even lingering into the winter, which, with the rose-like formation of the double flower, gave rise to its old name, the "Winter Rose." It was plentiful in southern Europe, and was well known to the Greeks and Romans, Pliny writing of it as "that rose which hath the stalk of a mallow and the leaf of a pot herb." The name Althea is from the Greek "althein" =to heal, and was given on account of the great medicinal virtues with which it, in common with all the mallows, was credited, and for which they were greatly valued by the mediæval herbalists. We read that they were "commonly and familiarly used" as antidotes for poisons, for the stings of scorpions, bees, and wasps ; and that "if a man be anointed with the leaues stamped with a little oil he shall not be stung at all." At the same time it was largely cultivated for its beauty, and was evidently an important plant in early English gardens. Gerard, at the end of the sixteenth century, tells us of many varieties, with both single and double flowers, "white or red, and of a deep purple colour, varying diuersly as Nature list to play with it."

HOLLYHOCK.

1. Terminal of the flower spike showing buds in various stages. 2. Later stages of opening buds.
3. Flower in profile. 4. Front view of the flower. 5. Calyx and epicalyx. 6. Showing leaf and
growth of branching main stem. 7. Stamens.

THE RHODODENDRON.

Nat. Ord., *Ericaceæ.*

THE Rhododendron is now so common in our gardens and in such variety of beautiful hybrids, that the original type is but little known ; but the derivation of the name, from "*rhoden*" = a rose, and "*dendron*" = a tree, points to its having been of a red rose colour, as does the early name of the Pontic Rhododendron, which it seems to have shared with the Oleander, the "Rose Bay." It was also known among the Greeks as the "Rose Laurel," or "Rhododaphne," and in later mediæval times Parkinson wrote of a small variety as the "Mountain Sweet Holly Rose," probably the small wild Alpine shrub which is still called the "Alpine Rose." It came to us from Pontus, in Asia Minor, now known as Armenia, in 1763 ; while the Azalea, with which it is so closely related, was brought from the same place thirty years later. It was so common as a wild shrub in its native country that it was said that the poisonous properties attributed to it affected the honey of the district, so much that the Romans refused to accept it as tribute ; and that at Trebisond Xenophon's army of ten thousand Greeks were poisoned from eating it, so that "the ground was strewn with their bodies as after a battle," though we are told that none of them died. It is now supposed that these hurtful properties may have been due to the Oleander, also a native, or to some other common wild herbs.

The Rhododendron is an evergreen shrub, growing from about five to fifteen feet in height, with thick knotted branches, much gnarled and twisted, and of a pale brown colour ; the older shrubs spreading over a great space, and forming dense masses of heavy foliage lasting all through the year. The oblong-lanceolate leaves taper towards the short thick stalks or petioles, springing in alternate order from the stem, and forming a whorled clustered growth at the extremities of the branches. They are of a thick leathery texture, with simple non-serrated edges, rather reflexed ; strong midrib and veining, and a smooth dull surface of a deep sombre green on the upper side, and paler glaucous colour, sometimes with a russet tinge, below. The whole growth is rather heavy and massive, but with firm vigorous lines, the clearly cut symmetrical leaves having much of the decorative quality of the laurel and the bay.

The large terminal clusters of blossom grow in corymbose racemes, the bud protected with pale green inbricated linear scales which are persistent, remaining at the foot of the radiating stalks in the centre of the flower-head. Each blossom has a small five-toothed calyx, a broad spreading campanulate corolla with five lobes, turning back in strong graceful curves and undulated at the edges ; a long style with projecting stigma, and ten stamens with rather large anthers—one of the chief botanical differences between the rhododendron and the azalea being in the double number of the stamens, which in the latter flower are only five. The variety illustrated is one of the modern hybrids in which the corolla, of a delicate transparent texture, is white, flushed at the edges with a soft lilac-pink, with splashes of pale green in the centre. Others give an infinite variety of colour, from pure white to numerous faint pink and lilac shades, deep rose and vivid crimson, with delicately pencilled markings of darker purple or madder brown ; but in all these the form and general structure varies very little. The flower is followed by five-valved capsules or seed-vessels, filled with numerous small brown seeds of irregular shape, ripening in August and September. The flowers and young leaf-growth appear generally in May and June, though one small dwarf variety sends out a delicate rose-coloured blossom in mid-winter.

It is a native not only of South-Eastern Europe and Asia Minor, especially of the Levant, Georgia, and the Caucasus, but also of the Malay Peninsula, India, and North America. It flourishes in mountainous districts, especially in the Himalayas, where it grows in great profusion. From these sources we have now a very large number of beautiful hybrids, many of those from the Indian shrub having a strong sweet scent.

To all students of plant-form the decorative qualities of the Rhododendron, with its large symmetrical masses of flowers, and strong vigorous leaf-growth, cannot fail to appeal ; it has especially a strong feeling of breadth and strength of line, combined with a certain looseness and freedom of growth, all of which are such valuable characteristics to the designer.

THE RHODODENDRON.

1, 2, 3. Successive stages of buds and opening flower.   4. Sections of blossom showing stamens and
pistil.   5. Stamen.   6. Pistil.   7. Stem showing joints.

THE MARROW.

Cucurbita pepo ovifera. Nat. Ord., *Cucurbitaceæ.*

VERY few of our plants are richer in decorative qualities than the various gourds, of which the familiar Vegetable Marrow, so often passed unnoticed in our kitchen gardens, is one of the finest. The strong vigorous lines of its thick stems and large spreading leaves, half hiding the big cup-like flowers, are beautifully contrasted by the most dainty delicate form in the young folded leaves and buds and slender curling tendrils, full of subtle drawing; while the big massive parti-coloured fruit is seen at the same time in all stages of its development, giving great variety of form with no effect of heaviness or monotony.

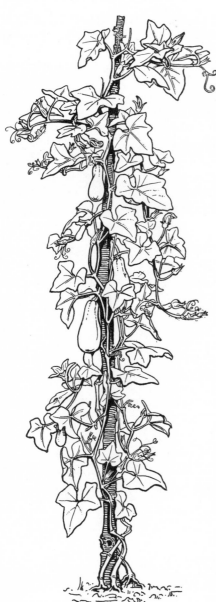

The long trailing herbaceous stems are soft and succulent, and much enlarged at the joints; they are studded with short prickly spines, and have a decided spiral twist which is a valuable characteristic to the draughtsman. The large leaves spring from the stem alternately, having long stalks, also set with short spines and slightly ciliated. The leaf when young is angular, with five clearly cut lobes, but when fully developed these are only slightly shown, and it takes a fuller rounder form. The palmate and netted veining is strongly marked, the edges serrated, and the surface billowy, with a rough downy texture. When fully grown it measures from twelve to eighteen inches in length, and at each node, from the axil of the leaf stalk, springs a flower and a delicate triply branching tendril.

The blossom is monœcious, having the two types with stamens and pistil in separate flowers, growing side by side on the same plant, and varying considerably in form. Both have the large funnel-shaped corolla with five spreading lobes, and a small calyx with narrow linear sepals; but while one flower is set on a long slender stalk, the other has the large ovary below the calyx which later developes into the fruit, and a thick short stem deeply furrowed. In the long-stemmed flower are five stamens with large anthers, in the other the lobed stigma with its short thick style. The buds are slender and tapering, with the corolla tightly closed, surrounded by the pointed sepals. In their earlier stages they are seen among the young folded leaves and tendrils, forming together a terminal growth full of detail and intricate form, clothed with long downy hairs which soften the outlines, and shed a delicate grey bloom over the fresh green. The flower is of a beautiful deep yellow, very mellow and brilliant, with thick outstanding ribs on the outer side of a pale green, continuing the colour of the stems, and contrasting with the stronger deeper tone of the large leaves.

The fruit varies in form and colour in the different kinds, but is generally of an oval form, slightly flattened at the base; some being entirely of pale green, changing to deep yellow as they ripen; others marked with splashes and broken stripes of darker colour. The gourds give a great variety of form, from the heavy "turk's cap" to the small pear-shaped fruits, with their irregular markings of yellow and strong dark green, and the small round "orange gourd," resembling the fruit from which it was named. Of all these the forms of the leaves differ slightly, some being rounder and simpler than others, but the general structure and habits of growth are practically the same.

The plant is prostrate, but grows well over a trellis, or trained to climb any upright support, grasping and holding with the curving tendrils, when the decorative qualities of the flower and fruit are seen to much greater effect than when trailing over a flat surface. *Cucurbita pepo*, the ordinary pumpkin, was brought from the Levant in 1570; other gourds are natives of southern Europe, Africa, and America; they grow freely in any corner of our gardens, flowering and bearing fruit in June, July, and August, but we read that "they joy best in a fruitful soil." In early English gardens the marrow was grown, with all the gourds, chiefly for its beauty, "because it climeth vp and is a couering for arbors and walking places, and banquetting houses in gardens"; and we are told that the fruit of it was "sometimes eaten, but with small delight." An old writer quoted by Gerard says that a "long gourde or else a cucumber being laid in a cradle by a yoong infant whilest it is asleepe and sicke of an ague, it shall very quickly be made whole."

1, 2, 3. Buds.   4. Pistillate flower.   5. Stigmatic flower.   6. Showing centre of pistillate flower.
7. Showing growth of stigma in centre of stigmatic flower.

Showing growth of the fruit.

REST HARROW.

Ononis camprestris.   Nat. Ord., *Leguminiferæ.*

THE Rest Harrow is one of the most delicately beautiful of our midsummer wild flowers. It is found in June and July, growing in tangled masses in the grass and weeds at the edges of the road-side, in rough pastures, and patches of fallow and waste ground ; forming big patches of pale colour, with a setting of sombre dull green foliage, interlaced with the tall straight stems of grass and herbage. And it should be understood that the upright grass stems shown with the blossom in the illustration are not included merely to form a decorative page, but also to show to some extent the usual growth and habit of the plant, with its scale among its almost invariable surroundings.

It is a small bushy herb or shrub, growing from one to two feet high, with upright branching hairy stems of a reddish purple colour. It has thick masses of finely cut foliage, and many short lateral shoots, terminating in long sharp thorns. The leaves are of oblong shape, or rather ovate, with serrated edges, a strongly marked mid-rib, and broad spreading stipules at the base of the short flexible stem, which often allows a downward droop to the leaf. Some of the lower are tri-foliate, or in threes, others solitary. They are thickly set in dense bushy masses, and the flowers are so plenti-fully grouped near the apex of the branch as to form an upright spike or panicle of blossom.

The flowers are of the usual form of the legumin-oseæ—like that of the pea. They are from half to three-quarters of an inch broad, the standard of pale rose pink, the keel touched with the same colour at its extremity, and the wings a delicate transparent white. The calyx is formed of five long pointed sepals, which develope into a deep setting for the soft hairy pod which follows the flower. This is of very characteristic shape, flat and round, with a curious downward curving beak.

The plant is a native found scattered over England, Scot-land, and Ireland. Another variety, often seen in our hedges, *Ononis arvensis*, is without thorns, and of more spreading growth ; and yet another, *Ononis reclinata*, is the small creeping rest harrow.

The name Rest Harrow explains itself. Gerard writes of it, " it is sooner founde than desired of husbande men because the tough and woodie rootes are cumbersome vnto them, by reason they do staie the plough, and make the oxen stande." Also, " Because it maketh the oxen whilest they be plowing to rest or stand still." From the same cause comes the old French name " Arreste Beuf." It was also known among old writers as the " Cammock Furze," " Ground Furze," and " Petty Whin." It was supposed to have medicinal virtues, and the young shoots were eaten by the ancients as a salad.

REST HARROW.

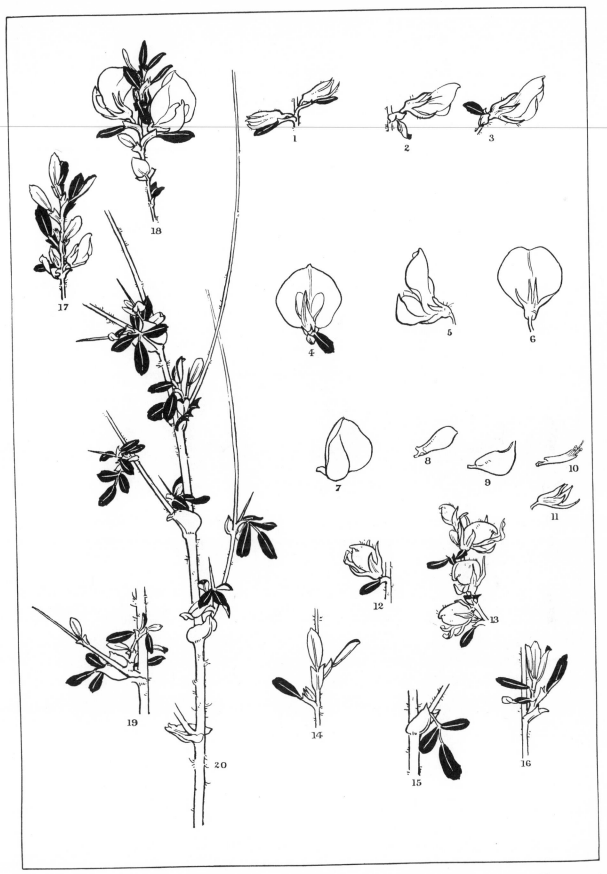

1, 2, 3. Stages of the bud. 4, 5, 6. Front side and back view of flower. PARTS OF THE FLOWER:
7. Standard; 8. Wing; 9. Keel; 10. Stamens and pistil; 11. Calyx. 12, 13. Seed pods.
14. Leaf growth. 15. Growth of leaf. 16. Branching leaf growth. 17, 18. Growth of buds and
flowers. 19. Spine. 20. Growth of main stem and branches.

THE ASH.

Nat. Ord., *Oleaceæ.*   *Fraxinus excelcior.*   *Fraxinus pendula.*

AMONG our trees we have no more beautiful example of plant-form than the Ash, called the "Venus of the Forest," so common in every English hedgerow and little wood.   By its very familiarity it seems to have escaped the close acquaintance and recognition which it deserves from students of design, not only for its beauty, but its eminent suitability for practical purposes.

It is one of the finest of our forest trees, and has been known to attain a height of ninety feet; but it varies greatly under different conditions.   Usually it rises with straight bare trunk to a considerable height before the branches are thrown out.   These spring in opposite pairs, but frequently only one survives, so that the growth has not a regular or symmetrical appearance.   The bark is smooth and of a pale ashen grey colour.   There are several varieties of the Ash, differing only

slightly in structure; but in the weeping *fraxinus pendula* we have a very marked difference in the manner of growth.   In the forest tree we find a generally upward growth of rounded curving stems, with more or less drooping foliage; and in the weeping variety, the long flowing lines and swaying pendulous branches, with heavily falling masses of leaves and winged seeds. The leaves are rounder and fuller in form and the keys in closer clusters than in the upright growth.   This variety is the one chosen for illustration, but the actual structure in both is almost identical, and the form is equally fine, though planned on different lines.

Fraxinus excelcior is one of our native forest trees.   *Fraxinus pendula* was first found in a field at Wimpole, in Cambridgeshire, about the middle of the eighteenth century.   From this tree it has been spread by grafts, and is now common in our gardens.   The leaves, which grow in clustered masses, are of the pinnate form, consisting of five, or sometimes six, pairs of opposite leaflets, with a single one as terminal.   They are almost sessile, and the way they spring from the split centre of the central stem, or petiole, should be especially noticed.   The edges are serrated, and the veining, and especially the mid-rib, strongly marked.   The clustered leaves are always found at the extremities of the branches; and then, not springing from the angles of the leaves, but directly from the bare branch beyond them, we find the heavy falling masses of the samara, or keys.   These are set on thin wiry branching stems; they are slightly thickened in the upper third, showing the hidden seed within, then flattened out into the blade-like surface of the wing.

The flowers are small and of no great account to the designer ; appearing early and never seen in conjunction with the fully developed leaves. They grow in small racemes of yellowish-green colour, having the two forms of pistillate and staminal blossoms ; sometimes one variety only on one tree, sometimes both. The opening buds of leaf and flower in early spring are very beautiful, and full of interest. Usually the tree is late in coming into leaf, and the foliage falls quickly after the first autumn frost, with only a slight change to a warmer brighter colour.

The beauty of form of the long leaves, growing in lightly clustered masses, and the falling samara, or keys, will be at once evident ; and the colour, simple and somewhat reserved, is also full of charm, with the quiet pure green of the leaves, contrasting with the yellower shade of the keys, which, as they ripen in late autumn, become almost golden. The long grey stems, telling lighter than the masses of foliage and the notes of dark purple—almost black—of the buds, complete a a scheme at once strong, unusual, and of great delicacy.

From the ashen grey colour of the branches the tree is sometimes said to have derived its name ; but more probably it is from the Saxon word " æse," a pike, for which the wood was used.

1. Opening bud.   2. Growth of the blossom.   3. Detail of the blossom.   4. Leaf growth.
5. Winged seed vessels.   6. Jointed branch.

THE PRIVET.

Ligustrum vulgar.   Nat. Ord., *Oleaceæ.*

THE old French " puine blanc " or " prim blanc "—" the little white shrub," gives the best descriptive name for the Privet, suggesting at once its low bushy growth and delicate white blossom, so like a miniature of the lilac, which is of the same order.

Although the delicately-cut flowers, if treated broadly and simply, are by no means unsuitable for decorative treatment, growing in big symmetrical masses, perhaps the simpler form of the berry is more amenable to most practical purposes.   The two are not seen in conjunction.

The plant is an upright bushy shrub, growing from six to eight or ten feet high, branching freely with opposite pairs of lateral shoots, and forming thick interlaced masses of olive-grey twigs and strong quiet green foliage.   The upper growth is erect and sturdy, sometimes rather angular, but the long flexible stems of the lower branches often take beautifully curving lines influenced by their search for light and air, and by the weight of the heavy bunches of berries ; such curving interlacing lines as may be of great value to the designer.   The pointed leaves, elliptic-lanceolate, grow in opposite pairs with short thick stems ; the edges are entire, the surface smooth, the mid-rib strongly marked, but other veining only slightly seen.   In early summer, if the shrub is left to its natural growth, uncut, each branch and lateral shoot is terminated by a pyramidal cluster of creamy

blossom, growing in a compound thyroid raceme.   Each separate flower is very small and delicately cut, the calyx tubular, four-toothed, the corolla funnel-shaped, having the tube much longer than the calyx, with a four-partite limb, forming a small cruciform flower.   Within the tube, and attached to its side, are two short stamens with small anthers, and in the centre a short style and obtuse stigma.   In late autumn the flower is followed by heavy clusters of round shining berries, of a deep purple colour, almost black, each berry containing two seeds.   The shrub being almost an evergreen, the dark green leaves, tipped after the first frosts with bronze, still surround the ripened fruit, forming a striking scheme of rich sombre colour which lasts far into the winter.

The Privet is a native in England, as in most of temperate Europe, and parts of Asia, Africa, and North America.   It is sometimes known as the " English Myrtle," and in Italy as " Olivella," or the " Little Olive."   Its old English name of " Prim-print " was probably given from its use in primly clipt hedges and quaintly cut figures in old gardens.   Although it is one of the commonest of our garden shrubs, it is in the woods and commons and in wild hedgerows, where it may be found growing freely and naturally, that we must look for its tangled masses of flowers and fruit in their full beauty, since the habit of our gardeners of cutting it into closely trimmed rectangular hedges effectually prevents our often seeing the luxuriance of its numerous clusters of creamy blossom, which shed a subtle penetrating scent on all the windward air ; or later the wealth of purple berries, which form a rich harvest for the birds.   In our gardens of to-day it is too often only a flat green wall ; it is only in the fields and waste grounds that we recognize it with its daintily poised masses of pale flowers as " the little white shrub."

THE PRIVET.

1. Buds.   2. Flower.   3. Section of the flower.   4. Stigma and style.   5. Calyx.   6. Berry.
7. Section of the berry.   8. General growth of flowers and leaves.   9, 10. Leaf terminals.
11, 12. Showing growth of the berry.

THE ARBUTUS, OR THE STRAWBERRY TREE.

Arbutus unedo. Nat. Ord., *Ericaceæ.*

A DOUBLE value seems to attach to those flowers which come to us in the late autumn and winter, breaking into buds and blossoms at the time of the sadness of falling leaves and general decay, when our gardens are comparatively bare. Of these the Arbutus is one of the most beautiful, and in November and December its delicate waxen blossoms may be found in abundance side by side with the rich crimson berries among the evergreen leaves ; this conjunction of flowers and fruit giving a wide variety, both of form and colour, which makes it not only a joy to all lovers of flowers, but also a most valuable subject for the practical purposes of the designer and decorative student.

Taking sometimes a low bushy form, sometimes rising as a standard tree to a height of from twenty to thirty feet, it is of strong vigorous growth, forming thick rounded masses of dark foliage, throwing strong deep shadows, and contrasting vividly with the pale warm brown stems and branches, which, from their habit of frequently casting their thin fibrous bark, shine light against the darker leaves. These are of simple ovate-lanceolate form, from one-and-a-half to three inches long, with short stems or petioles, the edges serrated, strongly marked mid-rib, but other veining not accentuated. Their texture is thick and heavy, the colour a dark sombre green, with the lower sides much paler. The tremulous pendant flowers grow in loose panicles, generally terminal, but sometimes springing laterally from the axil of a leaf. Each consists of a five-lobed calyx, a mono-petalous corolla from three-eights to one-and-a-half inches long, globose or ovate-campanulate, with five reflexed teeth, within which are the stamens, anthers, and stigma. They are very delicately formed, of a pale creamy colour, and the slender branching stalks are flushed with the warm red which runs through all the stems of the young branches as well as the older wood. The berries which follow the flower develope slowly, taking a whole year to mature, and only swelling and ripening, at the time of the flowers of the following season ; changing first from green to orange, then to their later brilliant crimson colour. They are about the size of a large cherry, with a rough surface, and each contains five cells enclosing several small seeds. The berry is sometimes eaten, but it is rough and unpleasant in flavour ; its specific name, *unedo*, from *unus*=one, and *edo*= I eat, implying that those who taste it will not take a second.

The Arbutus is found in Southern Europe, in Spain, Italy, and Greece, in England now, as in the time of the old herbalists, only " in some few gardens ; " but in the south and west of Ireland it is plentiful. Here it is judged by Loudon and some other authorities to be a native, while others state that it was introduced by the monks of Mucross Abbey. But another version of its origin is found in the old mediæval legend of the Irish monk, Bresal the singer, who followed Bishop Sedulius into Spain. And when he grew old a great longing seized him to return to his own country, and he bade farewell to the bishop and his fellow monks, and returned to his birthplace on the coast of Kerry. But he found himself a stranger among his own people, and after some time he was very lonely. And one day he was thinking of his friend the prior, whom he would never see again, and " he prayed for him with a great love." And he fell asleep and dreamt of his priory in Spain, and the plants and flowers surrounding it, the saxifrage with its little round leaves, and the evergreen Strawberry Tree with its scarlet berries. And at the same time the prior in Spain was thinking of Bresal, and saw him in a vision with his dream of his old home set in the Spanish garden, and he knew that he was sad ; so he prayed that he might have comfort, and that these things might be made real to him. And as he prayed Bresal awoke from his dream, and saw at his feet the saxifrage and at his right hand the strawberry tree, and he rose joyfully and his sorrow passed from him. And from that time the Spanish tree and the little Spanish flower have grown and flourished in Ireland.

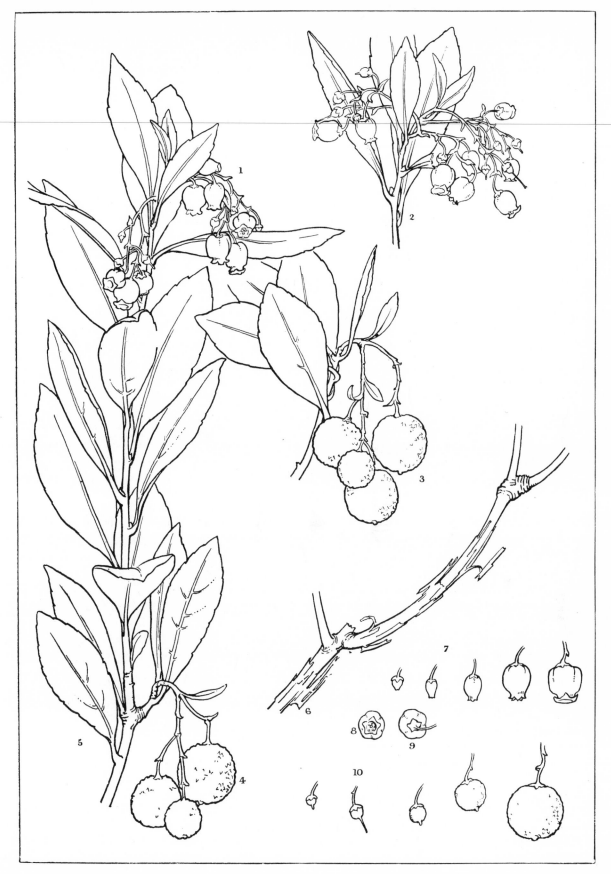

1, 2. Growth of flowers.   3, 4. Growth of berries.   5. Branch, showing growth and order of the leaves.   6. Stem, older wood.   7. Stages of bud and flower.   8. Front view of flower.   9. Back view of flower.   10. Stages of growth of the berry.

MOUNTAIN RANUNCULUS.

Nat. Ord., *Ranunculaceæ*.

AMONG our spring or early summer flowers, the Mountain Ranunculus is one of the finest from a decorative point of view. Its tossing golden balls, standing, on erect but flexible stems, above the thick clustering mass of the radical leaves, have a buoyant air which is peculiarly characteristic ; and that quality of looseness which is so valuable to the decorative artist. And through the whole plant runs a strong feeling of symmetry, not only in the grouping of the masses of leaves and flowers, but also in each separate part ; in bud and blossom, as well as in the richly varied form of the spreading palmate leaves, always perfectly balanced, yet full of variety and delicate drawing.

From the ground the roots send up a thick compact growth of long-stemmed radical leaves, each divided into five radiating partite segments, again subdivided into lobes, and crisply cut with sharp serrations at the edges. The beautifully netted veining is clearly marked, and the whole leaf is full of delicate curving form. The stem leaves are similar in character, but sessile, smaller, and some-

times of only three segments, these being of a more pointed, almost lanceolate, shape ; they are placed alternately on the stalk, which is sometimes branched from their axils. The stems are round and smooth, thick and sturdy, but flexible ; and though generally upright, sometimes take delicate lateral curves. They are of a soft pale green, lighter and brighter than the leaves, which are of a full deep, somewhat sombre, colour.

The buds, as they first appear, are of a fresh bright green, flecked here and there with touches of brown ; but, as they develope, and the sepals unfold, they take more and more a deep yellow colour, gradually lightening, till in the fully-opened flowers, they become perfect balls of pale gold. Lightly and loosely made, they consist of petaloid sepals of regular rounded form, concave in surface and with a curious clawed attachment. These open to disclose the full soft mass of anthers in the centre of the flower ; and as the sepals fall, these stamens and anthers are left surrounding the carpels, when the close relationship to the buttercup or meadow crowfoot becomes very marked ; as in the earlier stages of the blossom the resemblance to the anemone, with which it is also connected, is evident. The carpels remain after the anthers also have fallen, and grow to a considerable size before they open to shed the small purple-black seeds.

The plant of the Mountain Ranunculus grows from twelve to eighteen inches high, and occasionally it is even taller ; the flowers are from one to one-and-a-half inches across. It is one of our native plants, and is found also widely distributed over the temperate and northern parts of Europe. It was well-known among the early English herbalists. Gerard, in 1597, writes of it as "growing wild in almost every meadow in Yorkshire, Lancashire, and bordering shires of the North Country, but not in the south or west." Unfortunately it is no longer common among our wild flowers, though it is still found in the northern counties, and in Wales ; but it grows freely and plentifully in our gardens, flowering in May and June, and shedding its seeds in August.

Its name Troillius, is said to be derived from the old German word, Trol, a globe, and it is also known as the Globe Flower, Globe Crowfoot, Trol Flower, Lucken gowan or Cabbage Daisy, and Golden Ball.

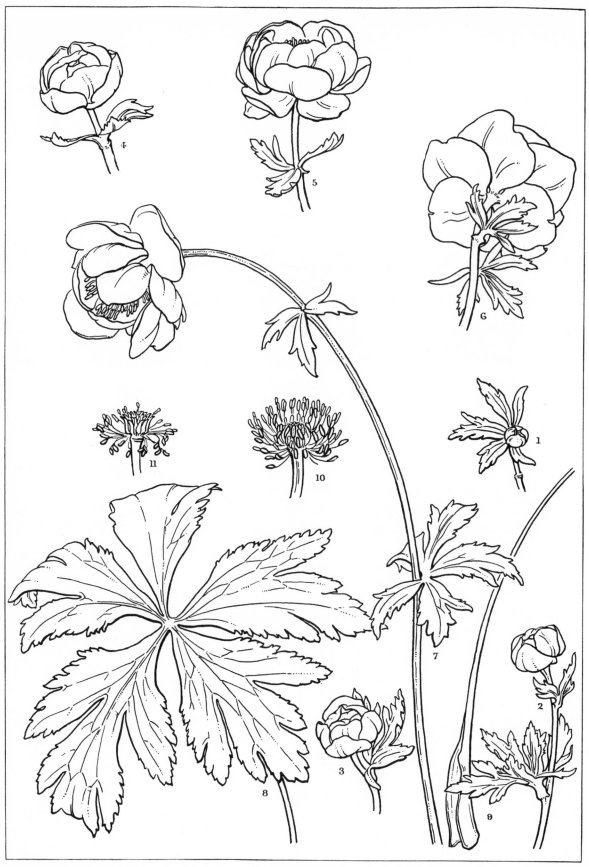

1, 2, 3. Successive stages of the buds.   4. Opening flower.   5. Flower in elevation.   6. Reverse of the flower.   7. Showing growth of flower and stem leaves.   8. Radical leaf.   9. Showing attachment of radical leaf stem.   10, 11. Early and later stages of the stamens and carpels after the fall of the sepals.

THE CUCKOO FLOWER.

Nat. Ord., *Cruciferæ.*   *Cardamine pratensis.*

"And by the meadow-trenches blow the faint sweet cuckoo flowers."—*Tennyson.*

WE could hardly have a more truthful and beautiful description of the Cuckoo Flower than Tennyson gives in these few words ; conveying not only its subtle delicate beauty, but also accurate details of its growth and environment. For it is by the marshy meadow trenches, in damp road-side hedges, in shadowy copses, and especially near the water's edge that we find the faint lavender of the cuckoo flower among the fresh dainty greens of early spring. It is probable that formerly, before the improved drainage of our pastures, it was much more plentiful in the meadow lands, for old writers likened the cuckoo flowers whitening the fields to linen bleaching in the sun. Shakespear writes of the "Lady's smock all silver white" ; and it is surmised that this old English name is derived from this supposed resemblance. More accurately it should be written "our Lady's smock," for it is one of the flowers which in mediæval times was dedicated to the Virgin, and used, like the marsh marigold or "mary-gold," so often found growing side by side with it, in the decoration of her shrines.

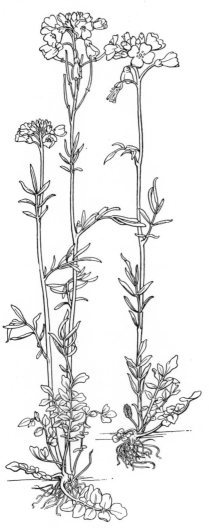

Among the tangled grasses the thready root of the cuckoo flower sends up a little cluster of radical leaves, pinnate, or having on a central stalk opposite pairs of leaflets, round, and quite different in form from those which spring from the upright stem. These have very slender curving strap-shaped leaflets, and are also of the pinnate form, but the growth is by no means invariably symmetrical ; and the order, and even the shapes of the leaves, are very irregular. The slender stem rises from the radical cluster with a great effect of straightness, yet always at the angle of each leaf changes its direction with a subtle curve. It is sometimes branched, each offshoot, like the main stem, being termin-ated by a corymbose cluster of blossom. The flowers measure from half to three-quarters of an inch across, and consist of a small calyx formed of four sepals ; a cup-shaped corolla of four petals of a pale lavender colour, or some-times white ; short stamens, with anthers, and a prominent style of pale yellow. The leaves are of a deep sombre green, and the whole effect of colour is reserved, yet very dainty and delicate.

The flower is followed by a long thin seed pod ; and as the blossoms successively open, and the stem grows, for a considerable length below the flowering terminal it is clothed by these pods, which are very characteristic and full of interest. As they mature they change their direction or bearing, adhering strictly to a fixed order or routine. When the flowers fade, and the petals fall, the pods are small and drooping ; as they gain in length they gradually take a horizontal position, standing out below the blossom in a protecting radiation of decided decorative value. Then, in their latest stage, they lift their heads and take almost vertical lines, nearly parallel to the stem, again protected by successive outstanding pods.

The plant is a native and very plentiful all over the British Isles. It is from twelve to about eighteen inches high, and flowers from April till June. Parkinson, in his "Garden of Pleasant Flowers," mentions several varieties, among them a double one. And John Gerard wrote of it as growing at "Hamptwich in Cheshire, where I had my be-ginning, which hath given me cause to christen it after my county fashion, 'Lady's smock.'"

THE CUCKOO FLOWER.

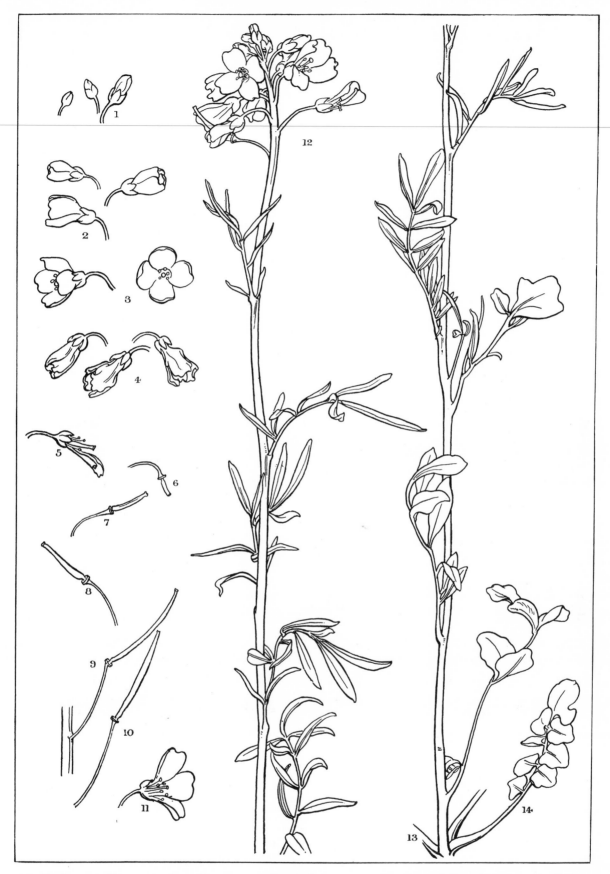

1. Buds.   2. Erect opening flowers.   3. Open flowers.   4. Prostrate fading flowers.   5. Calyx, showing stamens and seed vessel as the petals fall.   6, 7, 8, 9, 10. Stages of the pods, first prostrate, gradually more erect.   11. Section of the flower.   12. General growth of flower, stem and leaves. 13. Stem from the root, showing radical leaf.   14. Radical leaf.

THE YELLOW IRIS.

Iris Flavescens. Nat Ord. *Iridaceæ.*

FEW flowers have been more used in the decorative arts than the Iris, and since its straight flat leaves and somewhat severe growth do not tend to make it one of the easiest and most adaptable of motifs, it has often suffered considerably from mediocre renderings ; yet in the hands of the skilled worker, it has risen to a high level of simplicity and dignity, particularly under its most highly conventionalized and severe forms ; and few examples of plant form have added more to the beauty of all kinds of craftsmanship than the fleur-de-lys. It is found in old Egyptian and Persian art ; and in later mediæval times it was used continually, particularly in ecclesiastical work ; in carved stone and wood, in metal and stained glass, in frescoes and embroideries, and in heraldry. It is equally prominent, though not always with the same dignity of treatment, in our modern design, and the Japanese have used it largely, especially in their embroideries. The origin of the conventional form of the fleur-de-lys is supposed to have been the yellow water iris, which grew in profusion in the river of that name, but the actual structure of the flower varies very little in the many different varieties.

The Iris is a perennial plant springing from a running tuberous root with many slender radical fibres. The broad sword-shaped leaves are entire, sheathing at the base, and arranged with the edges overlapping each other ; the surface generally flat, though sometimes slightly channelled, and showing the straight parallel veining. The thick straight flower stem rises vertically, sometimes with one or two lateral branches, each springing from an enveloping spathe, and having terminal flower-heads. Each of these is enclosed in a scarious sheath, from within which two or three successive blossoms spring, the first having always the longest pedicel, and rising above those which follow. The flower is arranged in a triple whorl above the tubular perianth ; first the three large drooping segments, or sepals, then the three curved overarching stigmas, which, lying over the base of the sepals, conceal the stamens and anthers ; then rising above these three large upstanding segments or petals. In *Iris Flavescens* the colour is a very pale delicate yellow, veined with faint purple, giving a beautifully pencilled surface to the folded bud. The leaves are of a fresh brilliant green, having a delicate bloom, but not the glaucous bluish colour of the foliage of the purple flower. The blossoms as they fade change to a deep soft orange touched with a darker purple, forming a beautiful harmony with the pale golden yellow of the newly opened flower.

Iris Flavescens comes from the Caucasus, and only our native varieties will ripen their seeds in England, but in its congenial climate the flower is succeeded by the beautiful triple-valved seed vessel which is such a decorative feature of the plant.

By the Egyptians the Iris was considered the emblem of eloquence ; and in later mediæval times it was one of the many flowers sacred to the Virgin, and used in the decoration of her shrine. An old legend tells of a monk who lived, unlearned and despised by his brethren, but devout and offering daily many "Ave Maria's ; " and when he died, from his grave there sprang a yellow iris on which was pencilled in letters of gold the words "Ave Maria." On opening the grave the root was found to spring from the lips of the dead saint.

Many varieties of the Iris were cultivated by the old herbalists, not only for the blossom, but also for the medicinal properties of the root.

1, 2, 3. Successive stages of the buds.   4. Opening flower.   5. Flower.   6. Leaves showing the growth, one within the other.   7. Growth of leaf from the flower stem.   8, 9. Joint of buds and main stem.   10. Outer segment of the flower, with stamen and stigma.   11. Front view of the stamen.

THE NARCISSUS.

Nat. Ord., *Amaryllidaceæ.*

OF the same order as the Daffodil, the Narcissus shares many of its decorative qualities, and the growth and structure of the plant is to a great extent the same. It has the same bulbous root, the same sheathing envelopment of the young leaves as they first appear, and the same arrangement of the tightly-packed parallel blades in the sheath, enclosing the embryo flower-scape. Like those of the daffodil, the leaves are straight-veined, linear, strap-shaped; but broader and thicker, with bluntly rounded points, and of nearly equal width in their entire length, instead of tapering to their apex. The texture of the leaves is thicker and heavier, the surface slightly concave, and it is altogether of a stiffer, more severely upright growth, without the flowing sway of line of the daffodil; while the colour is darker and more sombre than the delicate grey green of that flower.

But the greater severity of the leaf growth is compensated and balanced by greater freedom and looseness in the structure and growth of the blossom. From between the parallel leaves rises a long upright stem or scape, straight and thick, on which the terminal cluster of buds is enclosed in a green spathe, which becomes scarious, a thin brown semi-transparent tissue, as the clustered flower-head developes. This consists of many separate blossoms, each on a long flexible pedicel or flower-stem. The buds are generally upright, but later, as the blossoms gain weight, these long lissom stems bend and sway with a beautifully loose pendant effect, which is one of the most valuable characteristics of the flower. Each blossom has a rather long perianth tube, rising from the flattened ovary, which gives the note of deep green at the base of the flower; six broad spreading perianth segments, often more or less channelled and crisply undulating; and a flat saucer-shaped crown, in the centre of which the six anthers are seen attached to the sides at the base by short stamens, and surrounding the more prominent stigma. The flower-stem rises in a vertical line from about fifteen to twenty-one inches high; the leaves, which grow in thick masses of heavy green, being of nearly equal length.

But though the narcissus is so rich in beauty of decorative form, a beauty which is especially valuable for all the practical purposes of the designer, perhaps its greatest glory is in its colour. The deep sombre green of the leaves, the pale creamy white of the delicate semi-transparent blossom, and the rich deep orange of the central crown, form together one of the simplest and at the same time one of the most beautiful harmonies in the whole range of floral colouring.

We have no native English narcissus; the plant came originally from France and Italy, and many of the beautiful varieties of our present-day gardens are due to modern cultivation. Its name, Narcissus, was derived from the well-known mythological tale of the youth who was changed into the flower.

1, 2, 3, 4. Opening florets.   5. Front view of flower.   6. Reverse of the flower.   7. Section of the flower.   8, 9, 10, 11. Successive stages of the flower head.   12. Bulb.   13. Leaf termination in profile.   14. Leaf termination.

THE BLUEBELL, OR WILD HYACINTH.

Nat. Ord., *Liliaceæ.* *Scilla nutans.*

EVERYONE is familiar with the Bluebell, or Wild Hyacinth, one of the commonest of our wild flowers, and one of the richest in grace and charm, both of colour and of delicate structure. It must not be confused with the Scottish Bluebell, known in the south as the Harebell. Its colour is well known to all, but certainly for its loveliness to be realized and understood, it must be seen growing ; its thick masses of rich purple stretching away under the pollard trees of some old wood, with intermitting patches of green, the fresh brilliant green of early spring, and blue again beyond ; and still beyond, green and blue ; a blue that is here purple, here almost grey, but always brilliant and warm in tone. Walking through these purple masses one finds here and there a white one, and again a pink, the latter of a sombre tone, and by no means plentiful. And looking into them as they grow one sees a maze of delicate straight stems, with the flowers, first upright, then as they gain weight, bending over in most beautiful curves ; and below them the thick carpet of leaves, some few erect, but generally prostrate, forming a background of strong vivid green. So the effect of a mass of bluebells is of a flattened undulating sea of heavy prostrate foliage, broken by numberless vertical lines of upright stems, and overhung by the dainty pendulous blossoms.

One must dig deep to find the root of the Bluebell, a small silvery white bulb, so delicate as to be quite in keeping with the beauty above ground. It is often many inches, perhaps from five to eight, or more, below the surface.

The flower is a long slender perianth of six segments. Within the tube, and attached to its sides, are six stamens and anthers, with the stigma and style springing from the ovary at the base. Each flower, or floret, has a short stem or pedicel, with two long bracts at its junction with the main stem, both bracts and stems taking the purple colour of the blossom. The flowers form a long terminal raceme, varying from three to six or seven inches in length.

The leaves are linear, or strap-shaped, long and so heavy that they are unable to support their own weight ; they are deeply heeled at their base, but flattened towards the extremity. They spring directly from the bulb, enveloping the central flower stem. In isolated plants they are often short, but in a thick growth they attain a very considerable length. I have measured some over eighteen inches long, and flower stems twenty-three-and-a-half inches ; and these were by no means exceptional.

The flower is succeeded by a beautiful triangular seed vessel, very decorative in form. It consists of three lobes, each filled with fine black seeds, and is still terminated by the persistent style, and supported by the long bracts at the base of the pedicel. It is sometimes as large as a small hazel nut, and though of considerable weight, it is generally erect, the whole raceme, when matured, having altogether lost the drooping character of the blossom.

1, 2, 3, 4, 5. Successive stages of buds and flower.   6. Sections showing the stamens, pistil, and ovary.   7. Bulb and roots, showing growth of leaves.   8. Various forms of the leaves.   9. Front view of flower, showing arrangement of the petals.   10. Seed vessels.   11. Section of the seed vessel.

PYRUS JAPONICA.

Nat. Ord., *Rosaceæ*.

OF all the large order of Rosaceæ, the Japanese Quince (Pyrus Japonica) is the most brilliant, striking the first strong note of vivid rose-red among the dainty whites, yellows and purples of our early spring flowers.

Coming almost before the winter is over, in February and March, the first blossoms often break from the bare stems before the leaves ; although the later flowers, more happily set among the opening clusters of tender vivid green, may perhaps be taken as the more natural and typical growth, as certainly they are more adaptable to most decorative purposes. It is a strong vigorous woody shrub, with thick knotted stems, throwing out, when left to its natural growth, long trailing branches thickly set with the brilliant clustering blossoms, interspersed at intervals, and always at the terminals, with spreading bunches of young foliage of a vivid green. The branches are set with long sharp thorns, and short thick lateral spurs from which the blossoms spring ; the bark is smooth and of a warm reddish-brown, but the stems, especially of the older wood, are rather angular and of a thick sturdy growth, while a certain character of squareness runs through the whole plant, both in buds and flowers, and in the rather wedge-shaped leaves.

On the short supporting spurs, lifting them away from the side of the branch, the flowers are set in clusters of two or three or more, very rarely do we find a solitary blossom. The calyx is composed of five blunt square lobes, the corolla of five broad concave petals, while the centre of the flower is a soft mass of long slender stamens and pale yellow anthers, set in two rows, which, however, are by no means clearly defined. The brilliant red of the petals runs over the calyx and short stems of the flowers, and even the young leaves. These, like the flowers, spring from the stem in radiating clusters at the joints ; they are of a blunt oval shape, sometimes almost square, smooth and glabrous on both sides, very slightly and irregularly serrated, with a thick strong mid-rib, but other veining not very clearly marked. They are attached to the branch by short thick stems, often appearing almost sessile. The shrub only occasionally produces its fruit in England, it is rather like an apple but longer, and having a strong square form instead of the soft roundness of that well-known fruit. It is of a deep green colour flushed with a deep dull red, and is ripe in October, when it is beautifully scented, but it is not edible.

Pyrus Japonica is a native of China and Japan, and was brought to England in 1815. It usually grows from five to six feet high, but is said to have reached fifteen feet against a wall. There are

several varieties, some in pale soft pink and creamy colours, and one with more double flowers, but the common well-known shrub is much the most effective. The beautiful simplicity of the form of its open blossom, buds and leaves makes it exceedingly valuable and suggestive to the designer ; and the Japanese have used it with great effect, especially in their embroideries.

PYRUS JAPONICA.

1, 2, 3, 4. Successive stages of buds. 5, 6. Front and profile views of flower. 7. Calyx and stamens after fall of petals. 8. Leaf growth. 9. Flowering branch with terminal leaves. 10, 11. Jointed stems. 12. Petals. 13. Stamens. 14. Fruit.

THE PURPLE ANEMONE.

Nat. Ord., *Ranunculaceæ*.

THE purple Anemone is one of a very large genus of perennial herbs, having a wide range of colour and considerable variety of form. Very early in the spring its tuberous root sends up a thick cluster of finely-cut radical leaves, springing singly directly from the earth, with no connecting crown above the surface of the soil. These spread and grow to a considerable size, each leaf being bi-ternate, divided into three segments, each of which are again sub-divided in three; they are pinnate and deeply serrated, with curled reflexed edges and strongly marked veining.

From this thick growth of delicately cut foliage the plant sends up a thick soft stem or scape, straight, unbranched, and bare, until, near the top, are placed three sessile leaves, forming a fringed cup-like involucre enclosing the young bud. This at first is quite concealed, but slowly emerges, a small globular shape, with tightly folded sepals of a pale green colour. Gradually the stem lengthens, lifting the bud above its protecting involucre, which becomes more spreading; and the petal-like sepals, brought into the light, taking the form of the absent petals, slowly change colour as they open from the pale green of the bud to the rich bluish-purple of the fully developed flower. They are very irregular in number, varying from five to twenty, the blossom being often semi-double, forming a cup-like perianth which, as the flower matures, changes from its close upright form to a more spreading shape, till finally the sepals are bent back below the head of the stem, and the thick

fringe of slender stamens and deep purple anthers surrounding the globular stigma, are plainly seen. The sepals then quickly fall, and the soft woolly seeds which the flower produces are generally quickly scattered by the wind. The plant sends up several blossoms, of a beautiful warm bluish-purple, very pure and bright in colour, accentuated by the darker anthers; while the stems and leaves are of a fresh delicate green, those of the involucre being splashed at their base with the warm rich colour of the sepals.

There are a great many varieties of the anemone. Beside the purple flower we have a white; numerous blendings of white and pink, and white and purple, some of pink and deeper red, and others of a brilliant scarlet; while one, the Pasque-flower, blossoming about Easter, has a soft grey down on the outer surface of the delicate mauve sepals.

Even in the sixteenth century they seem to have been very numerous, for we read of them as "without number, or at the least not known vnto anyone that hath written of plants," and "Euery newe yeere bringeth with it newe and strange kindes, and euery countrey his peculiar plants of this sort."

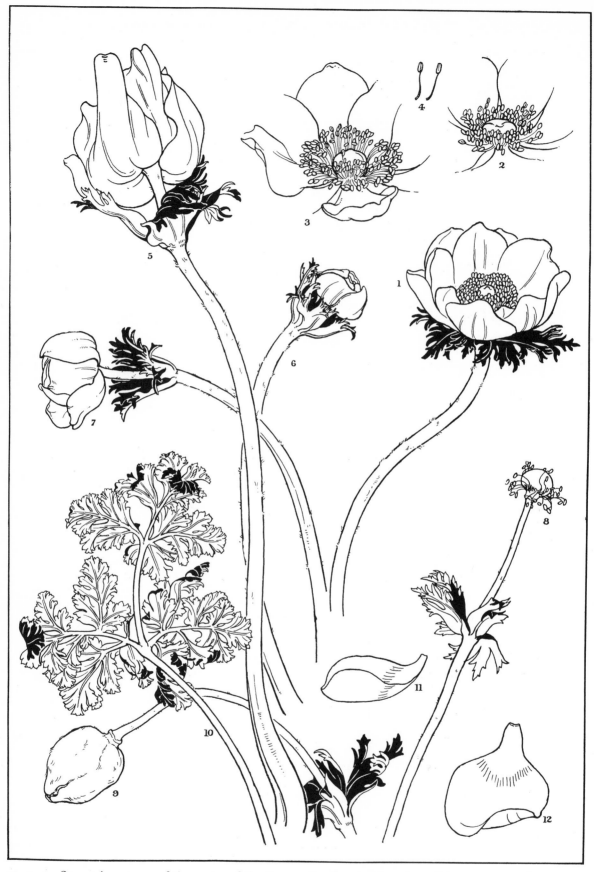

1, 2, 3. Successive stages of the centre of the flower, showing development of the stamens and various forms of the globular stigma. 4. Stamens. 5. Back view of the flower. 6, 7. Buds. 8. Stigma after fall of petals. 9. Later state of stigma. 10. Reverse of the leaf. 11, 12. Petals.

SALSIFY.

Nat. Ord., *Compositæ*.   *Tragopogon porrifolius*.

"Flora's clock, the Goat's beard."

STUDENTS of plant form will recognize at once the resemblance of the purple Salsify to the yellow Goat's beard, or meadow Salsify, so well known as a wild flower to all workers in design,—their close relationship is at once evident.   The form is almost the same, but in the cultivated variety it is stronger and larger, and the great decorative qualities of the wild flower are emphasized.   The long radiating sepals which project with a star-like effect beyond the blossom are yet finer, the beautifully characteristic forms of the buds and seed-heads are more pronounced, and the foliage is more abundant, and in strong upright growth, or long swaying lines.

And although it excels in form, it also has the great charm of beautiful delicate colour.   The leaves are of a very pale bluish green, often almost grey in the light ; and the stems a brighter, fresher tint, but still very delicate. The flower ranges from a pure warm blue, through all shades of mauve, to a rich reddish purple, or wine colour ; flecked on the disk with the golden yellow of the prominent pistils and styles, or as an old writer says, " dasht ouer as it were with a little yellow dust."

The Salsify is an annual, growing from eighteen inches to about three feet high.   From a tangled mass of broad blade-like, or linear, foliage, the strong smooth stem rises almost vertically, clothed with the enveloping leaves, and branching from their axils.   These leaves are long and slender, deeply keeled, and of very vigorous growth.   Each branching stem is terminated with a blossom, beneath which is a strongly marked, and very characteristic enlargement, and it is bare and free from leaves for some distance below it.

The flower takes the usual form of the compositæ.   From a decorative point of view it is very fine, not only in its starlike front view, but also in profile or elevation.   In the buds the long pointed sepals are folded over the florets, but as the flower opens they expand into a starlike radiation surrounding the purple rays, which again surround the small florets of the disk, in which the projecting yellow styles form notes of vivid colour. As the blossom fades the sepals again close over it exactly as in the bud, protecting the undeveloped seeds.   Later it again unfolds, and the beautiful head of winged seed gradually expands to a perfect ball of soft down, still with its long persistent sepals.   It is one of the finest of our decorative seed heads.

Like the Goat's beard, the flower is only open in the morning ; it unfolds very early, soon after sunrise, and closes at about twelve o'clock, from which habit it has received its quaint old English name, " Jack-go-to-bed-at-noon."   The duration of a single flower is very short, but the plants give a succession of blossom from early June till September.

The purple Salsify is now only found in our kitchen gardens, and its flowers are little known ; but the old herbalists of the sixteenth century evidently recognized its charm, for they mention it as being sought as a rare wild flower, found only on the banks of the river Chalden, in Lancashire ; and " sown in gardens for the beauty of its flowers everywhere."   It is still found wild in some few places in England, but it is questioned if it has not been introduced, and it is not generally considered a native, although the yellow Goat's beard undoubtedly is.

89

1. Bud.   2. Later stage of the bud.   3. Flower showing growth of stem and leaves.   4. Back of the flower.   5. Later stage of the flower with sepals closed, but showing the winged seeds within. 6. Head of ripened seed.   7. Seed.   8. Long outer floret.   9. Inner floret.

DIERVILLA ROSEA.

Syn. Weigelia. Nat. Ord., *Caprifoliaceæ.*

DIERVILLA is a native of North-Eastern America, China and Japan, and is a comparatively modern addition to our English gardens. The American variety, a yellow flowering one, was the first to be imported to Europe in 1739. It was brought by a French surgeon named Dierville to the botanist Tournefort, who named it after him—"Diervilla." But it was not until 1844 that the much more beautiful Chinese and Japanese varieties were introduced ; of which Diervilla rosea, a native of the former country, is one of the finest, and the one most generally grown.

It is a hardy bushy shrub, growing freely to about six feet in height, preferably in a moist, slightly shaded position. The many grey woody stems which rise directly from the ground have thin fibrous bark, are much branched, and generally erect ; but the lateral branches, after rising a considerable height, take a swaying or horizontal direction, and are more or less drooping at the extremities. They form a thick leafy growth of a deep full green, and in June and July are thickly set with the heavy clusters of flowers, springing in long wreaths from nearly every joint of the younger wood, and weighing down the slender arching stems with pendulous falling masses of foliage and blossom, often almost to the ground.

The leaves are of simple ovate-lanceolate shape, with well-marked veining, the surface undulating, and the edges, which are very finely serrated, rather incurved. They have short petioles, or leaf-stalks.

The blossoms have long slender stems of delicate green, with a small calyx of five narrow pointed sepals, a broad funnel-shaped corolla with five spreading lobes, within which the five anthers, on short stamens set in the sides of the funnel, are plainly seen, with the long style and projecting stigma. The buds, which are generally erect, are of firm characteristic form, and both they and the flowers are symmetrical and well-balanced. With the simple graceful shapes of the leaves, and well-

arranged distribution of the masses, the shrub seems to offer valuable and adaptable material, strong in decorative qualities, and full of interest to students of plant-form.

The colour rather suggests that of the apple-blossom. The flowers at the margin of the spreading lobes are of a very delicate pink, while the funnel and more or less of the lobes, or in some cases the whole blossom, is flushed with a darker purplish-rose colour, quiet and soft rather than brilliant in quality ; while the stamens and anthers, and projecting stigma and style, are of a creamy yellow. The buds are generally entirely of the deeper shade, and the whole clusters of flowers form a delicate parti-coloured mass, set in the deep soft green leaves, which also seem to take a clustering growth radiating from the blossoms.

There are several varieties of Diervilla, some with yellow flowers ; others in different blendings of soft creams and pinks, rose colour, and deep purple, and one modern hybrid with a pure white blossom ; while one has foliage of a warm golden green, and one variegated leaves.

DIERVILLA ROSEA.

1, 2, 3. Progressive stages of the buds. 4, 5, 6. Profile, reverse, and plan of the flower. 7. Leaf growth. 8. Showing general growth of the flowers. 9. Section of the flower. 10. Stamens and anthers. 11. Stigma and style. 12. Plan of the stigma.

SPIDERWORT.

Nat. Ord., *Commelinaceæ.*

OF the several varieties of the Spiderwort, the purple "Tradescantia virginica" is probably the best known, and may be considered the original type. It was this variety which was introduced into England in 1629 by John Tradescant, gardener to Charles I. As his friend, John Parkinson, writing in that year, tells us, "This Spiderwort is of late knowledge, and for it the Christian world is indebted vnto that painful industrious searcher and louer of all nature's varieties, John Tradescant, who first received it of a friend that brought it out of Virginia, thinking it to be the silk grass that groweth there, etc."

Spiderwort has much to commend it from a decorative point of view. Very individual, with characteristics of growth and structure quite its own, it is, perhaps, not quite like any other of our

common garden flowers. The strong lines of the stems, the long pliable linear leaves, and the heavy clustering cymes of buds and flowers, with their quaint triangular construction, are full of suggestion and adaptability. And in colour no less than in form it is striking and unusual ; the rich purple blue of the flowers contrasting vividly with the brilliant yellow anthers and the delicate glaucous greens of the leaves and stems, softened by the blending touches of purple on the segments of the drooping calyx.

"Tradescantia virginica" grows from one to two feet high. The stems are thick, strong and round, either simple or branched from the angles of the leaves ; generally erect, but sometimes bent with the weight of the heavy cymes of buds and flowers. The long linear leaves are broad at the base, enveloping the stem at the joints, and gradually narrowing to a sharp point at the apex. They are deeply keeled, with strongly marked mid-rib. When old, at about a third of their length, they droop at a sharp angle and become prostrate, the young foliage remaining erect. The name, Spiderwort, is derived from the supposed resemblance to the radiating legs of a spider in this spreading habit of the sharply-bent leaves.

The flowers grow in terminal or axillary cymes ; thick masses of buds, supported by two or three small bract-like leaves. Each blossom on a short pedicel or flower stalk consists of a persistent calyx of three sharp lanceolate sepals, a corolla of three broad flat spreading petals of a rich purple blue colour, and large brilliant yellow anthers set in bearded filaments. The thick rounded buds are closely packed together, but as the flower developes the stem lengthens and becomes erect, the open blossom standing above the clustered buds ; as it fades and the petals fall, it droops, and the closed calyx falls over the stem, taking again almost the form of a bud, but larger and more loosely made. The life of each separate floret is so short, opening at sunrise and closing in the early afternoon, that it was formerly known as "flower-of-a-day" ; but as the flower-head often consists of a great number of buds, and only two or three are open at once, it remains in blossom for a considerable time, giving a long succession of flowers during the early summer months.

Of the other varieties of the Spiderwort, some are much taller, from three to four feet high ; some of quite a dwarf habit. Their colour ranges from a deep reddish purple to delicate shades of pale warm blue or mauve, and one has a very beautiful white blossom.

SPIDERWORT.

1. Group of buds in successive stages.   2, 3, 4. Profile, reverse, and front plan of the flower.
5. Flowering branch, showing general growth of flowers, stems and leaves.   6. Buds
with undulating leaves.

THE RED CAMPION.

Nat. Ord., *Caryophillaceæ.*

In the spring and early summer, in the hedges of our country lanes, in woods, and especially in damp shady places by the waterside, we may see the numerous bright rose-pink blossoms of the Campion or " batchelor's button," the Rose Campion as it was formerly called.   It is said to prefer the shade, and it is certainly a woodland plant, but in sun or shade it flourishes everywhere, and its bright pink flowers may often be seen shining between the great stretches of bluebells or wild hyacinths, which cover all the ground in many densely shaded woody depths or sunny intersecting patches of felled underwood.

It is a perennial herb, having a tangled thready root and soft succulent stems, upright and branching ; not severely vertical, but with a flexible swaying grace in their long lines, while the flowers are sometimes slightly inclined, and the full grown leaves, heavy and flaccid, have a decided droop.   The lower leaves are obovate, lengthening into long petioles ; the upper, which are placed in opposite pairs on the stem, are sessile, oval or ovate, and tapering to a point.   The edges are entire, the veining strong and clearly marked, and the undulating surface, in common with that of the stems and buds, is ciliated or clothed with soft downy hairs, which give a grey tone over the deep dull green. The flowers grow in clustering cymes, flat round salver-shaped blossoms, generally of a deep purplish-pink, but varying in depth of tone, and often paler if growing in the shade.   The calyx is a long elliptical ovoid, narrowing towards the apex, and divided into five sharply cut teeth.   The corolla is composed of five petals, each deeply cut in the centre into two rather square lobes, and having at their base two acute lanceolate scales.   After the corolla fades, the ovoid-globular seed vessel becomes an important feature of the plant, still enclosed in the persistent calyx, which takes a fuller rounder form as the swelling capsule developes.   Altogether the Campion gives considerable variety of form and much beauty of line, and the dark grey-green leaves, soft rose-pink of the flowers, and the rich reddish-purple of the buds and stems form a scheme of colour which is at once strong and reserved, yet full of subtle values and delicate beauty. The plant grows from eighteen inches to about two feet in height, and the open flower measures from threequarters to one inch across.

The several varieties of the Campion were well known to the old herbalists, and esteemed, not only for their medicinal virtues, the seeds being prescribed " to be drunk in wine as a remedy for bites of scorpions or venomous beasts," but also for cultivation in gardens for the beauty of their flowers. John Parkinson writes, " There bee diuers sorts of campions, as well tame as wilde, and although some of them that I shall here entreat of may peradventure be found wilde in our owne countrey, yet in regard of their beautiful flowers they are to be respected and noursed vp with the rest, to furnish a garden of pleasure."

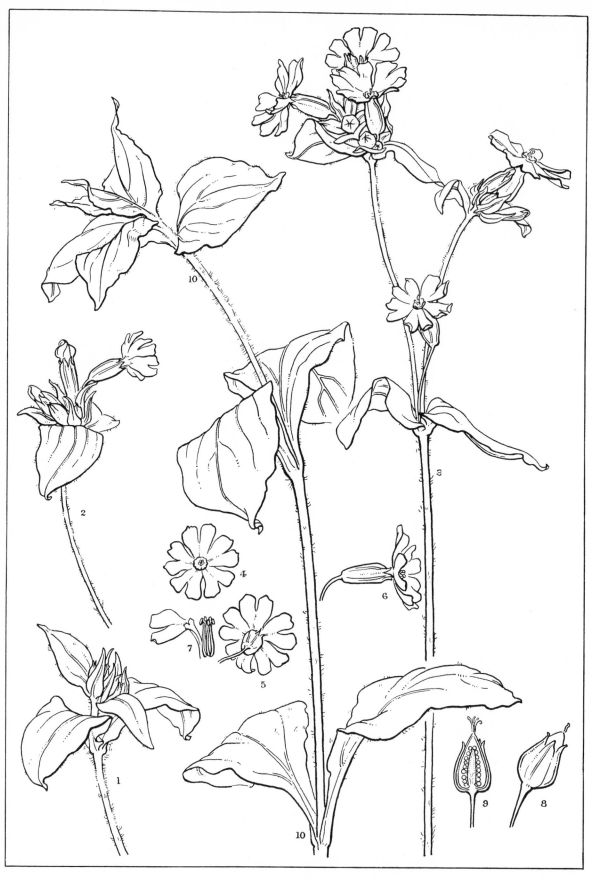

1. Bud.   2. Opening buds.   3. Showing general growth of the flower.   4. Plan of the flower.   5. Reverse of the flower.   6. Flower in profile.   7. Petal with stamens.   8. Seed vessel.   9. Section of the seed vessel.   10. Leaf terminal.

MEADOW CRANESBILL.

Nat. Ord., *Geraniaceæ*.

OF the several varieties of the Cranesbill, the Blue or Meadow Cranesbill is the largest, and perhaps the strongest in decorative qualities ; although all of them, especially the little Herb Robert, are rich in beauty and variety of form. The Meadow Cranesbill has the large open flower somewhat resembling the mallows, with which it is nearly connected ; and also, in common with all its species, the curious and very decorative long-beaked seed-vessel, from which it takes its name. It was formerly known as the Rose Cranesbill, from the size and shape of the blossom, "like vnto the smallest brier Rose in forme."

Each flower consists of a calyx of five pointed sepals ; five broad rounded petals forming a flat open cup-shaped corolla, from three-quarters to one inch in width ; with ten anthers on long stamens, thick and triangular at their base, forming together a closely-massed projecting group in the flower centre. After the petals fall the long beak of the seed-vessel gradually emerges from the encircling sepals of the persistent calyx. It consists of five separate carpels, which, as the seed ripens, split and break away from the base, rolling up towards the apex. This long seed-vessel forms a valuable decorative feature of the plant. The flowers grow generally as terminals, or laterally from the stem joints, in groups of two or sometimes three ; the buds as a rule drooping, the seed-vessels erect.

And while the flower and seed-vessel are both so eminently decorative, the leaf also is peculiarly rich in varied form. The stem leaves consist of three or five segments, and are opposite and sessile. The large radical leaves, set on long stems, have six segments, and these are again divided into numerous small pinnatifid lobes. These segments are very equal in size, radiating from the stem, so that the general outline of the leaf is of a circular mass. The curiously netted palmate veining is clearly marked.

The stems are perhaps rather weak, inclined to be prostrate at their base, then more erect, taking curious unexpected angles at the joints, where they are considerably enlarged. They are of a pale green colour, and soft downy texture, while the leaves are darker, of a rich quiet green. The flower is generally of a beautiful, warm, clear blue, but varies considerably under different conditions ; sometimes it is almost purple, sometimes nearly crimson, but always with the deeper purple anthers. The centre of the corolla is most daintily, very minutely, veined, with delicate crimson lines.

The Meadow Cranesbill is found growing wild in England, Ireland, and in Scotland, excepting in the extreme north. It is found in fields, hedges, and waste grounds ; and especially flourishes by the riversides, where it grows from eighteen inches to sometimes nearly four feet high, and flowers freely all through the summer months. Modern botanists speak of it as a native plant, but it should be noticed that the older herbalists, especially both Gerard and Parkinson, mention it as a "stranger" in England, and being imported from Central and South-Eastern Europe ; "not-withstanding I have it growing in my garden." The plant was supposed to have medicinal properties, and we read that "the roote heereof is singular good for such as after weakness crave to be restored to their former strength."

1, 2, 3, 4. Progressive stages of the buds.   5. Showing general growth of flowers and leaves.
6. Radical leaf.   7. Reverse of the flower.   8, 9, 10 11. Progressive stages of the seed-vessel.
12. Section of the seed-vessel.

THE CORN SOW THISTLE.

Nat. Ord., *Compositæ.*

AMONG our field plants the Corn Sow-Thistle is certainly very rich in decorative qualities. It is so familiar, and so commonly slighted as an undesirable weed, that perhaps because of its very abundance and familiarity its beauty is but little recognized. Yet few of our wild flowers are more perfect in graceful form, not merely in the flowers, but in the beautiful symmetry of the buds, and especially the closing blossoms, and in the variety of line in the tall upright stem and the long undulating spiny leaf. From the earliest stages of the bud to the fully opened flower, and from that again to the fully developed downy globular seed head, it gives a constantly varying succession of beautiful and symmetrical shapes.

It is among the tallest of the thistles, growing sometimes to a height of five feet, though sometimes only about eighteen inches. It is closely allied with the well-known rough or broad-leaved sow-thistle, which it very nearly resembles ; but the flower is much larger and grows more freely and loosely. Sometimes it has one simple stem, more often it branches from the axils of the leaves, and rises in long swaying lines, flexible, and swinging in the wind. Each branch is terminated with the corymbose clusters of large yellow flowers, and soft pale downy seed balls. The buds are thick, ovate, or barrel-shaped, tightly enclosed with the numerous overlapping segments of the involucre, which are of a dark green, and thickly covered with soft downy hairs. The flower has the structure of all the compositæ, the many spreading ray florets radiating from the centre of a flattened disk. The florets are very long and slender, square-tipped, somewhat irregular, giving the flower a looser effect than the smaller and more severely symmetrical blossom of the broad-leaved variety. It may almost be said to resemble some of the small yellow Japanese chrysanthemums, but the disk is flatter and more salver-shaped. As the flower fades the involucre again closes, but takes now a beautiful ovate-conical shape, very decorative, and quite distinct in form from the bud. It now throws off the withered yellow rays, which have changed to a deeper orange, adding a happy note of warm colour which contrasts with the bright fresh yellow ; and the soft grey down pappus of the winged seeds gradually emerges, and slowly expands into the perfect globular form, soon to be scattered by the wind.

The stem rises from a thin group of radical leaves ; it is smooth surfaced, slightly angular, but not winged, as are so many of the thistles. The radical leaves are narrow oblanceolate, runcinate, with broad lobes, varying very much in form and in the depth of their incision. The middle stem-leaves are similar in construction but simpler, and the upper are lanceolate and almost undivided. They are sessile, embracing the stem ; and all are more or less undulated, much serrated, and spinous at the edges. They are of a brighter fuller green than most of the thistles, and the stems are pale and fresh in colour. The pedicels and the stems, to some distance below the flowers, are covered with thick soft hair in common with the buds and involucre.

The Corn Sow-Thistle gives a long succession of blossom through July, August, and September. Its yellow flowers may be seen hanging above the surface of the fields of ripening corn, or springing from the weeds and grasses of fallow "foreacres" and waste ground. It is not a hedge or woodland plant.

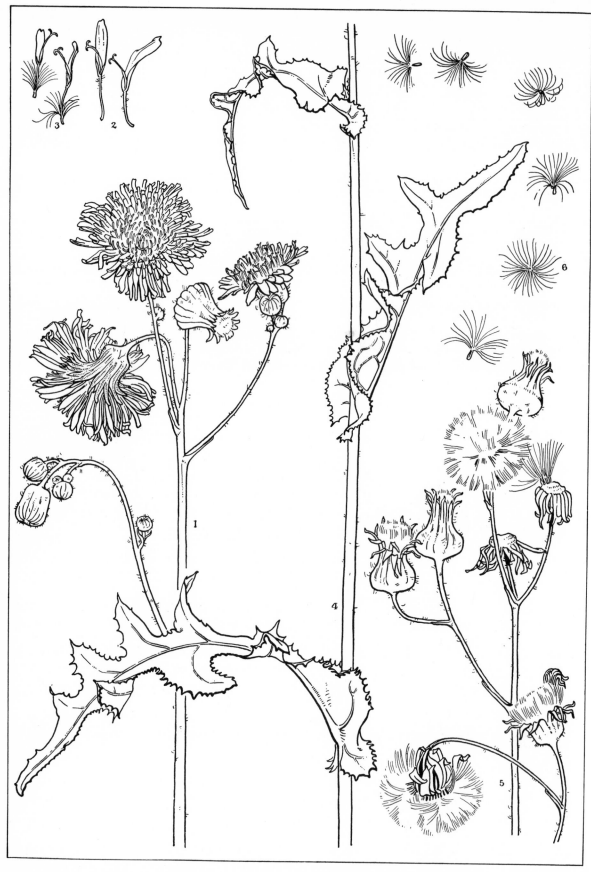

1. Flowering terminal, showing growth of buds and flower.   2. Florets in an early stage.
3. Florets later, with winged seeds attached.   4. Portion of lower stem, showing leaf growth.
5. Terminal in seed, showing seed heads in progressive stages.   6. Winged seeds.

THE FOXGLOVE.

Nat. Ord., *Scrophulariaceæ*.

"The Foxglove tall
Sheds its loose purple bells."—*Coleridge.*

SOMEWHAT severe in form, with its strong upright lines; reserved, but very rich in colour, with its sombre harmonies of purple and grey-green, the Foxglove is one of the most stately, almost regal, among our wild flowers. In the early summer months its tall spikes are common in many of our English hedgerows, in woods, on sandy commons, and on rough pastures and waste ground. It is found all over England and Scotland, excepting in the extreme north, and in some of the eastern counties; in Cambridgeshire particularly it is said to be absent.

It is a hardy herbaceous plant, growing from two-and-a-half to five, or even six, feet high. From a group of large radical leaves its strong thick stem rises; generally in a single upright line, but sometimes branched; the lateral shoots springing from the axils of the leaves, which are placed in alternate order. The radical leaves are of an oval-ovate shape, having long winged petioles, while the stem leaves are narrower in proportion, and their stalks are shorter. This difference in character is more marked as they are placed higher on the stem, until, just below the blossom, they are lanceolate in form, and almost, or sometimes quite, sessile. They are all of a sombre grey-green colour, and soft thick downy texture.

The flowers grow in a long upright raceme, each separate blossom set on a single peduncle, or flower stalk, below which is a long leaf-like bract. The calyx consists of five oval-lanceolate segments, divided almost to their base, very irregular, but, as a rule, having the lower segments longer and narrower than the upper. The tubular bell-shaped corolla is from one-and-a-half to two-and-a-half inches long, contracted at the base, and ventricose beneath. The reflexed upper lip is generally entire; the lower is in three short lobes, of which the lowest is the largest, and all are lightly ciliated on the inner side with short hairs. The colour of the corolla is a rich crimson purple, paler on the lower side, and spotted within with dark purple dots on irregular splashes of white. The stamens and anthers are hid in the tubular corolla, but as the flower fades, and succeeding buds above open, this is thrown off, leaving the capsule with its long style, set in the lengthening segments of the persistent calyx. As it ripens, this valvular capsule splits, shedding its brown seeds. So the ever-lengthening racemes open in a long succession of blossom and seed-vessels, all through the months of June and July, and sometimes considerably later. Another variety has white flowers, and yet another, a smaller plant, yellow.

The Foxglove is one of our poisonous plants. It was well known among the old herbalists. Blanchard mentions it as a remedy for fevers, and it was used in an ointment for king's evil. The origin of its curious name is very doubtful, but most probably it was originally "Folk's glove," or "the Fairie's glove," the name Folk's glove being found in an old list of plants of the time of Edward III. Another theory is that it is a corruption of "Fuch's" glove, so called after the German botanist of the sixteenth century. The glove-like shape is also recognized in the old French name, "Gants de Notre Dame."

1. Branching stem showing general growth of leaves and branches, with buds, flowers and seed-vessels.
2, 3. Transverse and vertical section of the seed-vessel.   4. Section of the corolla, showing stamens and anthers, ovary, style and stigma.   5. Stamen and anther.

JACOB'S LADDER.

Nat. Ord., *Polemoniaceæ.*

Jacob's Ladder, or *Polemonium Cæruleum,* is one of our hardy herbaceous plants often found growing luxuriantly in old cottage gardens, showing dainty patches of soft lilac blue or transparent white flowers, pendant above the rich green mass of the foliage. It is one of our most charming old fashioned flowers, giving a long succession of blossom in June and July, and taking its quaint name from the form of its pinnate leaves. Perhaps the first characteristic which strikes one is its charm of colour, but closer inspection reveals qualities of form also which seem of decorative value. The grouping of the loose spreading panicle of the flowers is often very happy, and the individual blossom, with its spreading open corolla with the prominent groups of anthers in the centre, is beautifully symmetrical and full of interest ; while the foliage also is suggestive and adaptable for practical purposes.

The plant is a perennial, growing, from a root which an old writer describes as " nothing else but as it were all threds," to a height of from eighteen inches to two-and-a-half, or sometimes three, feet. Its erect branching stems spring from a thick growth of radical leaves, each stem and branch terminated by a clustered spray or cyme of buds and flowers, forming a flat corymbose panicle of blossom. The stems take strong vigorous lines, they are hollow and angular, paler in colour than the foliage, and while taking slight changes of direction at the joints, keep generally to the vertical direction. The leaves are of the pinnate form, consisting of numerous pairs of leaflets with one as terminal, placed on a common central stem or petiole. As a rule they are alternate, but the order is so irregular that often they are found opposite or nearly so. Each leaflet is of ovate-lanceolate form, with edges entire, and firmly marked midrib ; and each is connected with the next by a narrow membranous wing running down each side of the petiole. The radical leaves are larger than those of the stem, having longer petioles, but the general construction is the same. The lateral branches spring from the axils of the stem leaves.

The flower grows with a slightly drooping habit ; the calyx, which is persistent, consists of five ovate-lanceolate segments, divided almost to their base ; the mono-petalous corolla is in five broad spreading segments, forming an open bell, from three-quarters to one inch across. It is of a very delicate transparent texture, and most beautiful colour, a warm soft blue, contrasting with the vivid orange of the five large prominent anthers. These are set on long stamens which are inserted in the base of the corolla, and form a conspicuous group, among which the style and three-cleft purple stigma are not very noticeable. After the fall of the corolla, the triple-valved seed vessel developes to a more globular shape, but still remains shorter than the segments of the persistent calyx, in which it is enveloped.

Jacob's Ladder is a native of Europe, temperate Asia, and North America. It is occasionally found growing wild in England, in York-shire, Westmoreland, Stafford, and Derby, but it is doubtful if it is not of garden origin. Old writers class it with the Valerians, as " Greekish or Greek Valerian," and by that name it is still known, although it has merely a very superficial resemblance, and is now placed in a different order. To quote John Parkinson, in the " Paradisi," "why it should be called a Valerian I see no great reason, for it agreeth with none of them in flower or seede."

1. Group of buds in successive stages.   2, 3, 4. Front, side view, and reverse of the flower.
5. Later stage of the flower.   6, 7, 8. Stages of the calyx and seed vessel after the fall of the corolla.
9. Flowering branch, showing general growth of buds, stem, and upper leaves.   10. Lower stem
with leaf growth.   11, 12. Radical leaves.

THE WINTER CHERRY.

Nat. Ord., *Salanaceæ.*

THE Winter Cherry, or *Physalis*, came originally from China and the Caucasus, though it is naturalized in North America, and was brought to us from Mexico. It is sometimes called the "Chinese Lantern plant," and certainly the big inflated calyx brings vividly to our minds the beautifully decorative forms of the Chinese lanterns, as we see them on a summer night, clean cut against the dusk, with their glow of brilliant colour, shedding no spreading rays of light to obliterate their clear outlines.

The plant illustrated is the smaller variety, not the larger *Physalis*, now so generally grown for the shops. It is rounder, daintier, and more delicate in form ; the foliage lighter, with more spring,

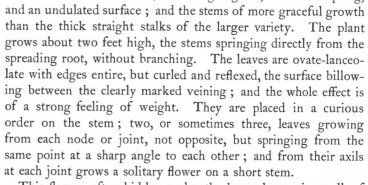

and an undulated surface ; and the stems of more graceful growth than the thick straight stalks of the larger variety. The plant grows about two feet high, the stems springing directly from the spreading root, without branching. The leaves are ovate-lanceolate with edges entire, but curled and reflexed, the surface billowing between the clearly marked veining ; and the whole effect is of a strong feeling of weight. They are placed in a curious order on the stem ; two, or sometimes three, leaves growing from each node or joint, not opposite, but springing from the same point at a sharp angle to each other ; and from their axils at each joint grows a solitary flower on a short stem.

This flower, often hidden under the heavy leaves, is small, of a greenish white or pale mauve colour, with rather prominent anthers, giving a touch of soft yellow in the centre. The calyx is five-lobed, campanulate, small at this stage, and giving no hint of its later extraordinary development ; the corolla monopetalous, also five-lobed, of a broad flattened bell, or salver, shape ; the edges much reflexed. The flower is followed by a round smooth berry of a brilliant orange colour ; and as this swells and ripens, the calyx, completely enveloping it, expands to the curious inflated form which is such a decorative feature of the plant.

In the earlier stages of this globular calyx it is green, inconspicuous among the leaves ; but as it grows larger it passes rapidly through a wide range of brilliant colours ; first to a soft rich golden yellow, then deeper orange, to scarlet, and at last to a vivid glowing flame-colour. And several of the berries on one stem ripening successively from the lower joints gradually upward, this whole range of brilliant tones, with all their intermediate gradations, may be seen at the same time on one plant ; while the leaves also, slowly changing the heavy monotonous green of their summer growth, fade softly to rich maize-coloured yellow, broken and flecked with touches of the soft purple that flushes the stems. Later the leaves turn brown and fall, but the brilliant fruit remains on the stem, till rain and frost slowly dissolve the tissue of the membranous husk, and the red berry is seen through the delicate interlacing net work of the skeletonized brown veining.

The Winter Cherry flowers in July and August, and the berries mature so quickly that the fully developed fruit may be seen on the lower stem, while at the extremity we may still find flowers and buds. The berry of this smaller variety is said to be edible. It was formerly known for its medicinal properties, and was called also the red night shade. Its modern name, Physalis, is from physa, or physalis, a bladder.

THE WINTER CHERRY.

1, 2, 3, 4. Buds in progressive stages.   5, 6, 7. Profile, front, and back view of the flower.
8. Showing growth of flowers and leaves.   9. Showing growth of the fruit enclosed in the enlarged
calyx.   10. Section of calyx showing the fruit within.   11. Section of fruit showing the seeds.

PHLOX.

Nat. Ord., *Polemoniaceæ*.

ONE of the commonest of our old-fashioned flowers, the Phlox has been very little noticed by students of plant-form, although its large clustered blossom and the simple undulating leaves seem to have many qualities of practical value to the designer, particularly in its well-massed grouping. In July and August, and even late in the autumn, it may be found in nearly every old-fashioned country garden, forming great patches of pale delicate colour and shedding a subtle penetrating scent.

The tall herbaceous stems rise from the root almost vertically to a height of from two to three feet, as a rule without branches, until the first lateral flower-stalks of the terminal panicle of blossom, although occasionally some leafy shoots may be seen springing from the axils of the leaves below. There are no radical leaves; those of the stem are placed in opposite pairs at short intervals from just above the ground up to, and into, the spreading truss of blossom. They are of simple oblong-lanceolate shape, tapering towards the apex; the edges entire, with long straight mid-rib and well-marked veining, and the undulating surface of smooth glaucous texture.

The blossom consists of a branching panicle forming a thick bushy mass of buds and flowers. Each has a tubular calyx with five narrow pointed teeth; a corolla, also tubular, but forming a flat salver-shaped flower with the five broad spreading lobes, the overlapping of which causes a curious wheeled effect, which is a strongly-marked characteristic of the blossom, and which is noticeable in the spiral folding of the bud, and especially in the opening flower, as shown in the drawings of detail. The stamens and style are not very evident, being placed in the tube of the corolla, which quickly falls, leaving them attached to the persistent calyx. The growth of the panicle differs in the many varieties, some being much more lightly and loosely grouped than others, while that with the white flower is close and less spreading.

Growing very freely and luxuriantly, each tall straight stem of the plant being terminated by one of these large flower-heads, they form rich masses of pale blossoms in a wide range of delicate colour, pure white, or white with subtle blendings of faint lilac and lavender, soft pink and rose, these quiet old-world shades seeming much more consistent with the true character of the original type than the more brilliant varieties of salmon and rich red which are now produced by modern gardeners.

The Phlox is a native of North America and Asiatic Russia; in spite of the derivation of the name from the Greek " phlox " = a flame, seeming to imply a brilliant flower, the pale coloured blossoms must be considered the primitive type; and the plant originally bearing the name is supposed to have been one of the Agrostemna, a genus of vividly coloured flowers, also natives of North America, but bearing no resemblance to it. It is not known when or how the name came to be transferred, but the Phlox, as we designate it to-day, does not seem to have been known in mediæval English gardens, and there is no reference to it in the old herbals.

1. Buds in progressive stages. 2. Plan of opening flower. 3. Plan of flower. 4. Flower in elevation.
5. Reverse of flower. 6. Flowering spray, showing general growth of leaves and blossoms. 7. Spray
with terminal buds. 8. Branching stem, showing joints. 9. Sections of calyx and corolla.

KERRIA JAPONICA.

Nat. Ord., *Rosaceæ.*

In Kerria Japonica we have another of the many beautiful plants for which we are indebted to the East, particularly to China and Japan. In 1700 it was brought to us, as its name implies, from the latter country, probably by a botanist named Kerr, who was for a time superintendent of the Botanical Gardens in Ceylon, and a great collector of plants; and in whose honour it received its name "Kerria." It is very hardy, and its beautiful golden flowers, set in the fresh bright green of the young leaves and stems, may now be seen in spring and early summer in nearly every country garden.

It is an upright shrub, with long slender flexible stems, smooth and brittle, springing directly from the ground, at first vertically, but with more or less swaying lines above. The thin twig-like lateral branches break from the main stem alternately and spread in a rather horizontal direction, often taking a pendulous downward droop at the extremities, forming thick masses of tangled falling growth. At the same time it is full of lightness and elasticity, with a character of buoyancy and airiness, and nothing heavy in its delicate structure. Though quite erect and able to stand alone, it grows in greatest luxuriance against a wall, or with some other sheltering support, and reaches a height of about six feet, or sometimes rather more.

The leaves, placed in opposite pairs on the stem, are of a beautiful simple shape, ovate-lanceolate, the edges rather deeply and clearly cut and serrated, with strong straight mid-rib, and clearly marked feathered veining, standing out rib-like on the reverse. They have short curved stems, with small linear stipules, and the slender flower stalks, from one to two inches long, spring from their axils.

At first sight the blossom might be mistaken for a chrysanthemum instead of one of the Rosaceæ; it has a strong superficial resemblance and all the decorative qualities of that much-used flower, including the valuable one of great looseness and freedom; but a glance at the reverse, and the five broad spreading petals at the back, dispels the illusion. It consists of a small five-toothed calyx; these five broad concave petals common to the rosaceæ, and supporting the numerous slender finely-cut ones which make up the soft mass of the centre of the flower, in which the stamens and style are concealed. In the bud the outer petals are folded over each other; as they open the flower gradually spreads, till finally it takes almost a globular form, when the petals slowly loosen and fall. Both stems and leaves are of a fresh bright green, the latter paler and slightly hairy on the reverse, while the blossoms are of a deep golden yellow, beautifully pure and vivid in quality. It flowers very freely, successive blossoms springing from each joint at the extremities of the branches with a wreath-like effect, forming a blaze of brilliant colour in sunny corners of our gardens. And in its form, with its branching spreading growth, the simple symmetrical leaves and tossing loosely-formed flowers, full of interest and delicate detail, it offers valuable material for many of the practical purposes of the student and decorative artist.

There is also a single variety, of quite equal beauty, but taking more of the well-known general form of the rosaceæ order.

KERRIA JAPONICA.

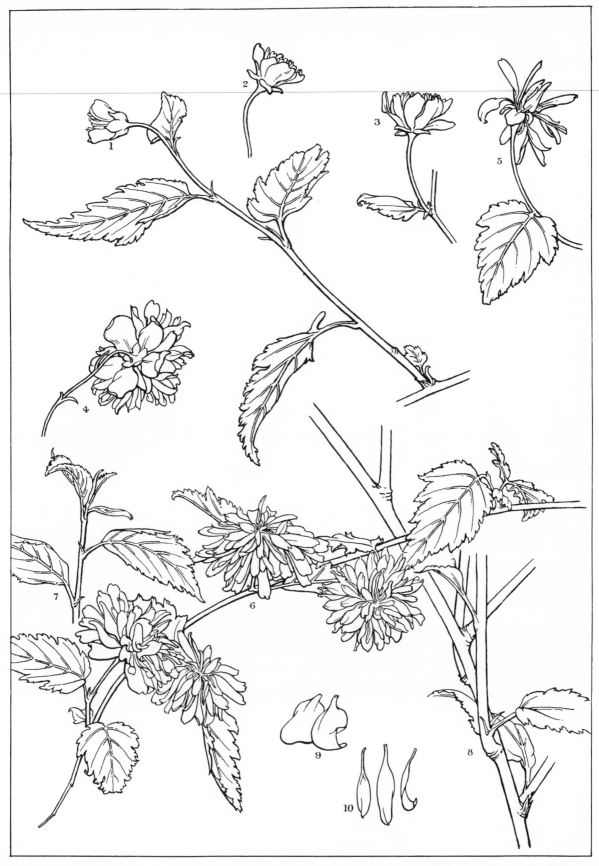

1, 2, 3. Opening buds.　4. Back view of the flower.　5. Later stage of flower with petals falling.
6. General growth of leaves and flowers.　7. Terminal leaf growth.　8. Main stem with joints.
9, 10. Various forms of petals.

SWEET SULTAN.

Nat. Ord., *Compositæ*.

ALTHOUGH the Sweet Sultan of our gardens was not originally a British plant, one is struck at once with its close resemblance to the Greater Knapweed (Centaurea Scabiosa) so common in our hedges, which seems at first sight almost identical with the purple variety. It is, however, more delicately formed, the leaves more finely cut, and its branching succulent stems are thicker and softer than the tough fibrous stalks of the Knapweed.

Seeking it out in the old English herbals, we find no record of it in those of the sixteenth century. Gerard, in 1597, does not mention it, but his follower, Parkinson, in 1629, writes of it as a kind of cornflower, "another stranger of great beautie, and but lately obtained from Constantinople, where because (it is said) the great Turke as we call him saw it abroad, liked it, and wore it himselfe, all his vassals haue had it in great regard, and hath been obtained from them by some that haue sent it into these parts." From this origin it was called the "Sultan's Flower," hence our Sweet Sultan; also the Turkey blush Cornflower. Later writers state, however, that it was a native not of Constantinople but of Persia, and the yellow-flowered variety, introduced later, in 1683, of the Levant. The plant was evidently well known to the ancients, and by them it was credited with medicinal virtues; its name, Centaurea, was given it from the legend that it cured a wound in the foot of the centaur, Chiron, caused by an arrow of Hercules.

It is a hardy herbaceous plant, growing from eighteen inches to about two feet high, branching freely with numerous lateral axillary shoots, each terminated by a long-stemmed blossom. Perhaps its chief characteristic is the great delicacy of its form, the foliage finely and intricately cut, the young growth sometimes almost feathery, forming a pale filmy mass of silvery grey-green. The larger leaves are very irregular, broad, spatulate, and unequally lobed, the edges sharply but unevenly serrated, yet the effect of the whole is well balanced and symmetrical. The netted veining is clearly marked, the colour a deep sombre green, contrasting with the delicate tones of the young foliage, and the texture thick and heavy, the whole of the older leaf growth having a decided droop.

The flower is of the usual structure of the compositæ, formed of numerous separate florets. An important feature, and one of very considerable decorative value, is the large globular involucre of scarious bracts, each delicately fringed at the apex, and closely overlapping each other. All the florets are tubular and toothed, the outer much larger than those of the central disk, which form a soft compact mass of tiny fringed petals. It is noticeable that in the purple-flowering plant the blossom is rather looser, the pointed teeth of the floret narrower and much longer, and the foliage also is more feathery and finely cut than in the yellow variety.

Altogether, with the beautiful symmetrical form of the flower, the adaptable lobed and serrated leaves, with the filmy undergrowth of the young foliage, few plants offer greater facilities to the designer than this "stranger of great beautie" now so well known in our gardens.

1, 2, 3, 4. Buds.   5, 6, 7. Opening flowers.   8, 9, 10. Different views of the flower.   11. Calyx.
12. Section of calyx, showing the seed.   13. Seed.   14. Outer florets of purple flower.
15. Outer florets of yellow flower.   16. Centre florets.   17. Part of the main stem, showing
growth of leaves and branches.

CLEMATIS VITICELLA.

Nat. Ord., *Ranunculaceæ.*

THE Clematis illustrated is one of the Viticella, or Vine Bower, of which there are several varieties, varying in colour from a pure warm blue to deeper purple and a soft rose colour. It is quite hardy, and grows freely and luxuriantly, producing a thick tangle of interlacing growth, running over old walls, trellis, or rock-work, or climbing the trunks of trees and hanging from the branches ; throwing out innumerable beautiful bell-shaped flowers, and forming, against the green, a rich mass of soft hazy colour in many otherwise bare corners of our gardens. It has quite a different growth to the large Clematis Jackmanni ; alert and springy, with slender wiry stems, instead of heavy and drooping. It is not one of the numerous modern hybrids, but a very old and distinct species, a native of southern Europe and western Asia, brought to England in 1569. It seems to be identical with that clematis known to the mediæval herbalists as the Great Bush Bower, other varieties being the "Virgin's Bower," red and purple "Lady's Bower," etc. ; these plants being known as "Bower plants," from their use in covering arbours, and arches in trellis walks, in old gardens.

It is a perennial, with slender herbaceous stems, much branched ; having on the young flowering growth, at each joint, simple opposite leaves, though on the lower stems they are often compound, of three or five leaflets. The growth is straight and direct, and the solitary leaves being sessile, there is no grasping of the twisted stems as in so many of the clematis, when the leaf stalks almost take the place of tendrils. The leaves are oval-lanceolate in shape, with simple unserrated edges, and curiously netted veining.

The tapering buds have clearly marked characteristic lines, taking beautiful campanula forms as they gradually expand, while the fully-opened blossom appears as one of our most perfect examples of a bell-shaped flower, pre-eminent among the clematis for grace of form.

The flower consists of four sepals, strongly and triply keeled, with undulating edges, taking the form of the absent petals, and radiating from the thick mass of stamens, which form a well defined projecting circle in the centre of the flower, surrounding the incipient carpels. After the sepals fall, these grow to a considerable size, and give fresh interest and variety to the form, being slightly feathered, but not to the same extent as the wild "traveller's joy."

The outer side of the sepals is covered with a soft down, giving a cool grey tone, which contrasts pleasantly with the warm rich colour of the inner surface, while the stamens in the centre are of a pale greenish yellow. The leaves are of a deep quiet green, while the rich purple of the flowers runs down and blends with the colour of the stems, forming together a beautiful harmony of strong reserved colour.

1, 2, 3, 4, 5. Successive stages of the bud. 6, 7. Opening flowers. 8. Back view of the flower. 9. Part of main stem, showing general growth of leaves and lateral flower branches. 10. Joint of main stem. 11. Showing growth of stamens. 12, 13. Later stages of stamens.

THE AZALEA.

Nat. Ord., *Ericaceæ.*

THE Azalea, perhaps the most brilliant of all our flowering shrubs, is very widely distributed, and comes to us from the Levant and the Caucasus, from India, Java, China and Japan, and from America. That from the Levant, from Pontus, known as the Pontic Azalea, illustrated here, was the first to be brought to England in 1793, and is still the commonest of our hardy varieties, and one of the most beautiful, although there are now a great number of hybrids which more or less resemble it. The first of these was produced at Hammersmith, and others in private gardens in England; later the Belgians, in the neighbourhood of Ghent, have cultivated it with very fine results.

It is so far hardy that, given a favourable soil, it grows and flowers freely in any sheltered position, forming in early summer, in May and June, rich masses of pure vivid colour, a glow like sunlight of soft deep orange, contrasting with the fresh tender green of the young leaves; while other varieties give a wide range of creamy white, amber, pink, and deeper flame colour, yet always with a subtle quality of softness and delicacy. And when the flowers have passed, in late autumn, the leaves, changing to all shades of mellow gold, crimson, and deep bronze, are hardly less beautiful and wonderful, until they fall.

The shrub grows generally from four to about six feet high, though occasionally the older plants under favourable conditions may be taller. The slender stems are much branched, knotted, and twisting in sudden curves and unexpected angles, forming at the extremities a bushy growth of delicate upright grey twigs, arranged more or less in broad horizontal planes. Both the flowers and the clusters of leaf-growth are terminal, springing only from the young green wood; and in this variety both have a curious clammy quality which is not found in the American Azalea.

The slender leaves are of simple oblong-lanceolate form, unserrated, with the edges much reflexed, especially in the young foliage, the veining clearly marked on the undulating surface, the texture delicate, softened by fine ciliating hairs. They have short stalks, and the entire growth of leaves and young green stem comes from a bud enclosed in an involucre of long linear scales, which are persistent, folding back over the branch at the well-marked junction of the old and new wood, each leafy shoot forming a complete and symmetrical growth, full of interest and grace.

The blossom forms a broad spreading corymbose raceme of long-stemmed flowers radiating from a common centre, the outer being the first to open. As in the leaf-growth, the brown scales which enveloped the bud are persistent, and remain in the centre of the flower-head. Each flower has a small five-toothed calyx, a long slender tubular corolla with five reflexed petal-like lobes; three above, where the soft maize colour is broken with markings of deeper orange, and two below, curling back in close curves. From within the tube the long thread-like stamens and style, supporting the anthers and flattened round stigma, sweep outwards in long graceful upward lines, forming a prominent and characteristic feature of the flower. For delicacy of structure, symmetry, and balance, the Azalea, both in its leaf-growth and in the blossom, may perhaps be said to be unsurpassed in plant-form, having all the decorative qualities of the honeysuckle, with a stronger, fuller flower. At first sight the resemblance of the two is noticeable, but they differ in many structural points, and are not of the same order.

THE AZALEA.

1, 2. Buds.   3. Front view of the flower.   4. Reverse of the flower.   5. Profile of the flower.
6. Calyx showing growth of stigma and style, with stamen and anther.   7. Leaf growth.
8. Jointed stem.   9. General growth of the blossom.

THE OLEANDER.

Nat. Ord., *Apocynaceæ. Nerium Oleander.*

WITH its vigorous alert growth of branch and foliage, full of graceful line, and its clustered masses of rose-like blossoms, the Oleander seems to excel both in form and colour, and to be especially rich in the decorative qualities which are needed by students of design. It is a tough woody shrub, in this country usually five or six feet high, but in its native soil often growing to fourteen feet, or even more. It is very graceful in its growth, light and vigorous, with slender stems full of swaying movement ; the young terminal shoots generally erect, but sometimes, when in blossom, drooping, weighed down by the heavy clusters of flowers. This feeling of weight is one of its most marked characteristics.

The brown stems, covered with rough bark, rise erectly, generally throwing out branches at a short distance from the ground ; always three branches from each joint, although often only one or two may survive. They spring from the axils of the leaves, which also are set in triple whorls, this triple order of branch and leaf being very strictly kept. The slender lanceolate leaves are from four to six inches long, with edges entire, a strongly-marked mid-rib, and rather short petiole or stem ; with the exception of the mid-rib the veining is not emphasized. The upper surface of the leaf is of a dark sombre green, the lower paler.

The flowers grow in heavy terminal clusters, technically in racemose cymes, pedicellate, on short stems. The calyx is small, and rather weak, composed of fine-toothed sepals. The corolla funnel-shaped, of broad spreading petals delicately curved, filla-metose, cut or fringed at their apex, as shown in the detail sketch. The colour is a most delicate rose pink, streaked and broken with white, and gradating to a creamy tone as the long claw of the petal passes into the calyx tube. The whole contrasting very beautifully with the sombre deep green of the leaves, and the paler glaucous tone of their lower surface. There are several varieties of the shrub, in some the blossom is single, and one has a very beautiful white flower.

The Oleander is a native of south-eastern Europe, especially of the Levant, and all the shores of the Mediterranean, of sub-tropical Asia, and of Japan, and seems essentially eastern in character. In England it is a greenhouse shrub, and not very familiar, but it is one that well repays study, not merely for its delicate beauty, but also for its valuable decorative qualities. Although not largely cultivated, it is not of recent importation, and was well known to the mediæval herbalists as the " Rose Bay," a name it shared with the Rhododendron. It was a favourite flower with the Greeks and Romans.

1. Flower in profile, showing growth from the stem.   2. Buds.   3. Showing triple growth of flowering spray.   4. Leaf growth.   5. Joints of main stem.   6. Petal.
7. Calyx, showing growth of petal.

BARLEY.

Hordeum vulgare. Nat. Ord. *Graminaceæ.*

NICHOLAS CULPEPER, writing of Barley in 1657, says, "the continual usefulness hereof hath made all in general so acquainted herewith that it is altogether needless to describe it ; " and it seems, indeed, so well known that everyone must be familiar with its graceful bearded ears and tall pliable stems, and has watched the swaying beauty of a field of the ripening grain set in wave-like movement by the summer wind.

In structure it is much the most decorative of any of our corn-bearing grasses. Its tall slender stem varies in height from two to about three feet. It is erect but flexible, clothed with the long blades of the leaf-sheaths which spring from the tough knots at short intervals. These leaves have numerous parallel linear veins, and taper to a sharp point at the apex. The different stages of growth are full of interest and give beautiful variety of form ; at first the spike is enclosed in the sheathing blade which protects the undeveloped ear, then the long awns are first seen projecting from the top ; and, forced by the swelling grain, it gradually opens and the soft green ear is seen within ; finally the sheath is cast off and the long awns spread out on either side with a radiating effect. The ear is at first erect, but as the grain gains weight it gradually bends over, until when fully ripe, it is turned quite back against the stem.

The ear is bi-lateral ; flat, with two parallel rows of grain, not square as in wheat. It is formed of successive groups of three flowering spikelets, of which only one is fruitful, producing the one grain with its long awn. These groups are alternate on the central rachis, but owing to the curving of the ear the alternation is often not clearly seen, and the grains may appear almost opposite. During the flowering season the pale yellow stamens are seen projecting from the spikelets, but the two small feathered stigmas are sessile, and are not evident.

In colour the Barley is very delicate ; the stems and blades in the unripened state are of a fresh bright green, with a soft grey glaucous bloom, while, as it ripens, it bleaches to a very pale straw colour, much lighter than the golden straw of wheat or oats ; forming in its intermediate stages unexpected subtle contrasts of pale green and blue, and delicate whitening straw.

Barley, or *Hordeum*, is said to have been the first cereal cultivated by man, and among the early Egyptians it was their most important grain. It was also largely grown by the Romans, both for their horses and as food for men. The gladiators were known as Hordiarii from their use of it while training, and it was the principal food of their army, from which fact comes our word " horde." In later mediæval times barley bread was largely used, though we read that it was considered " unwholesome for melancholy people," and an old writer, Bodeus à Stapel, traces the derivation of its name *Hordeum* from " hordus " = heavy, because barley bread was heavy. It had also many strange medicinal uses.

The Celtic " bara " = bread, gives us the modern name barley, also our word " barn," and from the old English " bere," a slight alteration of the Celtic, we have " beer," from the use of barley for malt.

Barley is now largely grown in Southern Europe, where it grows quickly, only about nine weeks elapsing from seed time till harvest, and yields two annual crops, cut in spring and late autumn.

1, 2, 3. Successive stages of the green ear. 4. Ripened ear. 5. Root. 6. Single grain with bearded husk. 7. Grain with husk removed.

THE SNOWBERRY.

Nat. Ord., *Caprifoliaceæ*.

THE Snowberry, also known as "St. Peter's Wort," one of the commonest shrubs in English gardens, is a native of North America, found principally in the mountains of Mexico. It is one of those that give at the same time both flower and fruit, and is a beautiful example of simple clear-cut form and delicate colour. The soft pure green of the foliage, touched after an early frost with splashes of warm purple brown; the exquisite white of the clusters of berries, gradating from their earliest stages through various shades of pale green; with here and there among them the bright pink of the small flowers which are seen side by side with the fruit; form a beautiful and unusual scheme among the warm reds and browns of late autumn. And on a single spray we may often find bud and flower, and every stage of growth of the berry.

The many upright branching stems spring directly from the ground to a height varying from four to eight feet, taking strong swaying lines. The upper branches are sturdy and erect, the terminals, though set with heavy clusters of berries, remaining upright; others take more or less sweeping lateral curves; while the maze of pendulous undergrowth, the thin thread-like stems weighed down by the terminal bunches of fruit, falls in straight vertical lines.

The opposite leaves, of beautifully simple ovate form, have short curved stalks, the edges entire, and the mid-rib and veining strongly and clearly marked. Sometimes the surface is flat, often it takes billowing curved planes.

The flowers consist of a tiny calyx of five sepals, a small cup-shaped five-petalled corolla, the outer side of a bright rose pink, the inner white, enclosing the stamens and style. They grow in loose irregular racemes, as terminals or axillary. The globular ovary at the base of the calyx quickly increases in size, berries of one cluster in all stages of development being found before the terminal flower of the raceme falls, some being as large as a hazel nut. The shrub bears very freely numerous starry clusters of pure white, which remain long after the fall of the leaves.

THE SNOWBERRY.

1, 2. Growth of blossoms.   3. Plan and elevation of the flower.   4. Main stem with branches.
5. Branch showing growth of flowers and berries.   6, 7. Terminals with berries.
8, 9, 10.   Terminals with berries, from drooping undergrowth.

THE SPINDLE TREE.

Euonymus Europœus.   Nat. Ord., *Celastraceæ.*

NONE of our autumn berries are more decorative in form, or of more vivid and unusual colour, than the brilliant rose and orange capsules and seeds of the Spindlewood, " the fruit that is a flower." It is a native of England and the south of Scotland and of most of temperate Europe, and although it is not one of the commonest of our hedge bushes, it is not rare.   It is found principally on chalk, in woods and hedgerows, growing about ten or twelve feet high, while in cultivation as a standard tree it occasionally rises to about twenty-five feet.   It seems to have been formerly more frequent than at present, its wood being largely used, as its name implies, for making spindles, and among many other purposes for skewers, from which it was known as " prickwood ; " it was also called the Gatteridge, or Gaitre Tree, from a Saxon word meaning a cover, in allusion to the shape of the overhanging capsule, and the French name, " Bonnet de prêtre," is from the supposed resemblance to a priest's cap.

The bushy branching stems are of a pale ashen grey colour ; sometimes rather erect, but more often, especially in the lower branches, of a graceful pendulous growth, twisting and shooting out at sudden unexpected angles.   The leaves placed in opposite pairs are of simple ovate-lanceolate shape, with finely serrated edges, and strong clearly marked veining.   In May or June it sends out a long-stemmed cyme of two or more greenish-white cruciform flowers, quite small and unobtrusive ; springing not, as is more usual, from the axils of the leaves, but directly from the woody stem.

The flower is followed by the beautiful clearly cut four-lobed capsule, which, at first green, slowly changes to a deep rose pink, very bright and pure in colour, and later opens and spreads to show the four ripening seeds within.   These are of a brilliant orange with a slightly roughened dead surface. The berries, or capsules are pendant, but do not fall heavily, often taking rather a lateral direction, and the growth of the whole plant is very light, alert and springy, with a scattered-all-over effect, rather than with any decided massing.   The capsules are late in coming to maturity, taking their brilliant rose colour in October, and opening only in November, when the leaves are already showing all shades of subtle golden and bronze tints before they fall.

The Greek name, " *Euonymus*," signifies " of good repute," but the tree does not seem to have been greatly valued except for the wood, while the leaves and berries were considered poisonous. We are told by an old writer, quoting Theophrastus, that " This shrub is hurtful to all things, and the fruite heereof as he saith killeth ; so do the leaues and fruite destroye Goats especially."

THE SPINDLE TREE.

1. Flowering spray, showing general growth of the blossom. 2. Showing growth of the blossom from the stem. 3. Buds. 4. Front view, reverse, and profile of the blossom. 5. Calyx and capsule after fall of the petals. 6. General growth of leaves and berries. 7, 8, 9, 10, 11, 12. Successive stages of the berries. 13. Jointed stem.